INVISIBLE

The Story of Diversity, Equity, and Inclusion in the United States

CAROLINE KING, PHD

The picture that started my journey.

authorHOUSE®

AuthorHouse™
1663 Liberty Drive
Bloomington, IN 47403
www.authorhouse.com
Phone: 833-262-8899

Published by AuthorHouse   06/28/2023

ISBN: 978-1-6655-7864-6 (sc)
ISBN: 978-1-6655-7863-9 (e)

Print information available on the last page.

To all the beautiful colors of the rainbow that make up our world and to my muses, Penelope and Oliva, who lead with love. And to those who have been overlooked and marginalized and fought back, risking their livelihoods and putting themselves in harm's way to pave the path forward.—thank you.

*The war we have to wage today has only one goal
and that is to make the world safe for diversity.*

- U Thant

Contents

Foreword

Dear Reader,

Thank you for walking or scrolling past the other books and picking up this one. I hope it adds value to your life and helps you think about people in terms of our similarities instead of our differences, how people are individuals and do not easily fit into a pre-categorized group. Through the process of putting this book together and launching my company, which is focused on diversity crisis management and diversity education, I have come away with this singular piece of knowledge: namely, that every person has a story and many of them are quite similar. So, when you meet a person who you that may appear to be ignorant, uneducated or some other label, take a moment to think about their perspective and how it feels to be labeled or stereotyped.

I rewrote this forward many times trying to capture just the right sentiment. Hopefully that comes across! Through my life experiences, I have come to believe that most people are very similar, whether it's our interests, talents, or concerns about our loved ones, there is a lot that unites us and plenty of common ground.

Last year an individual accosted my child's class at their elementary school. This enraged me as it would anyone else, but after taking some time to reflect, I realized it was highly likely this bitter old man had his reasons for hating people who are different from himself. Regardless of how misguided those reasons are, I began to understand it must be sad for him to live in such a small, lonely space. In the course of doing my research for this book, I spoke with many people from diverse populations. Some expressed gratitude that we are now discussing this issue. Many others, however, expressed severe frustration and skepticism that a book like this could make a measurable difference. After years of feeling marginalized and "less than," those feelings are certainly understandable. My hope is that, through education and genuine, open discussion, this book will encourage others to make actionable changes and pave the way forward.

For those of you who do not identify as being diverse or in a minority group, I challenge you to think about how it would feel to walk in someone else's shoes. What would you do if you worked for a company for 10 years and repeatedly got passed over for promotion? How would you feel if you saw less-qualified individuals receive the promotion you deserved, time after time? What if your child came home with a broken heart because somebody said unkind things to them about a perceived difference? These experiences make up who we are and who we become. It truly works both ways, exerting a negative impact on the aggressor as well as the person who is being minimized. What makes somebody so scared of a difference they feel the need to devalue someone? These are questions I believe we should be asking ourselves, and each other. After many years of frustration and feeling marginalized, I decided to educate and share my experiences with adults, children, businesses, and schools. My company is built on the principle that all humans have value and deserve respect.

As I researched, wrote, and interviewed others, it became a labor of love. My perspective is a unique one and worth sharing as it sheds light on many of the beliefs and insights you will find throughout this book. A recent ancestry test showed me that I am over 97 percent African, placing me at a high risk for heart disease. The result was puzzling because it was contrary to what I know about my lineage, so naturally I questioned its accuracy. It also made me think about my heritage and life experiences. This made me the person I am today and, if these experiences have the potential to break down some of the barriers that come from living in a diverse, yet not inclusive society, I decided they were worth sharing.

I was adopted when I was five weeks old by a white family. They raised me the best they could, but my childhood was not a story of how love has the power to conquer everything, including the rampant racism of the 1980s. During this period, I assumed the constant racist jokes were just going to be a part of my daily life. Likewise, I was excluded at every conceivable opportunity. My first 20 years were a long and painful journey of learning things the hard way. It was many years before I was finally able to embrace my authentic self as an African American female living in a white-dominated world.

My goal with this book is help people understand they are perfect as they are and are not meant to be any other way, no matter your race, nationality, creed, culture, gender, neurodiversity or sexual orientation. Equity and inclusion are human rights issues. This is intended as a call to action and my hope is that we can take it upon ourselves to become better educated on how to live an inclusive life and promote equity and equality within our spheres of influence.

As I researched and wrote this book, I asked others to share very personal, raw insights and stories about their experiences. Thus, it's only fair I share some of mine. Early in life, I realized I wasn't "black" enough to be accepted by the African American community where I grew up. Also, I was obviously not white, so I realized fitting in would be difficult. After enduring a troublesome, lonely childhood during the 1980s and early 1990s, I learned the fine art of assimilation. This can be a dangerous game to play, as it's easy to lose your identity and sense of personhood. I found that if I acted, sounded, and looked the way a particular cultural group wanted me to, life was a little bit easier. What I didn't realize was that every minute I participated in this behavior made me lose a piece of myself.

In my case, I was an African American living with a Caucasian family. The white American culture was attractive for me because I idolized my mom and my two sisters. Recanting my story would not be complete without including my brother, as he had a profound influence on my life. Like me, he was an African American who was adopted by a white family. Unlike me, he was born in the late 1960s, which were obviously not the best times for African Americans or people of color here in the US, although the work of Dr. Martin Luther King and the Civil Rights Act were steps in the right direction. My brother was considerably darker in complexion than I am and the fact that this is relevant is very unfortunate.

Due to a variety of reasons, including the cultural zeitgeist surrounding the time in which he was born, as well as a number of behavioral traits that would be attributed to ADHD nowadays, it's impossible for me to comprehend his struggle. However, he was a beacon of light and a talented actor, a fun big brother and a kind soul. He embraced a negative aspect of the stereotype that was pervasive concerning African Americans back then—violence, drugs and what the media would have deemed "animalistic" behaviors at the time eventually led to incarceration. I witnessed how cultural biases extinguished the light inside of him. The sadness and outrage over what he was forced to deal with is something I struggle with every day. Putting my empathy aside for a moment and channeling the frustration into educating others has been a positive way to deal with it. My brother was a brilliant and beautiful soul but he was thrown away because of the color of his skin. The outcome of those experiences was that I focused on becoming as 'perfect' as I could be in the eyes of others. My goal was to become invisible. As a child, I played the violin and piano, had perfect grammar, and was a classically trained ballet dancer. It was not uncommon for people to tell me that I was the whitest black person they knew. Sadly, this was meant as a compliment.

I can only speak for my own experiences. I felt like I was a member of an inferior race and I was told I would never amount to anything. My most outstanding achievement would be to not have multiple children by different fathers by the time I hit 15. I began receiving these messages when I was five or six years old; they became part of my DNA.

By the time I was in my mid-twenties, I was telling everyone who made ridiculous comments to take a long walk off a short pier, as my mom would say. These comments are now called micro-aggressions. At the time, I did not have the language to describe why I could no longer have those relationships in my life. I just knew I was tired, and it did not feel right. I was tired of hearing, "I'm not talking about you; I'm talking about the other black people." The ridiculousness of the statement was little comfort because, guess what? I am the other black people.

Another pivotal moment occurred when I heard Michelle Obama discuss how she was teased in school because she earned good grades and was told that meant she was acting "white." That was the most incredible thing I had ever heard, and it was a game-changer for me. I began to wonder if there were others like me who were also lonely and feeling like outcasts. Were they also watching the first lady and thinking to themselves, "I've never heard that before. This is incredible." Was it okay if I spoke using the grammar I was taught me in school, sang Broadway shows nonstop in the car and read books from Ernest Hemingway? Was it ok to just be me and not fit into a stereotype?

Michelle Obama transformed my life on her first day as First Lady. During a media visit to an elementary school, she flipped a switch inside of me. What I had perceived as flaws suddenly turned into strengths; it just took me 20-plus years to get there. I was immediately conscious and awake: it was simultaneously exhilarating and excruciating. For the first time, I began studying the country, looking around and taking things in, thinking about where I came from and where I was going. I conducted historical research and sought out my peers to have real but uncomfortable discussions. Along the way, I met some incredible women. Learning about their experiences was both disconcerting and reassuring. I wanted to yell "Ditto!" at the end of every sentence in our conversations because many of our stories were very similar.

In the 1990s, I would often check the box indicating I was "white" on job applications to get interviews. I was confident that I could get the job if I got the interview—I could talk myself into any position. If I checked the box marked "African American," however, I would never receive a callback. I honed the skills required to land the positions I needed to advance in my career—becoming a master at blending in and making people feel at ease around me and never questioning authority, keeping my head down, and working at least twice as hard as my coworkers. I gained confidence by putting myself through college and earning my Ph.D. while working to climb the corporate ladder.

This might not seem too horrible at first glance, but I paid a steep price. Having to adapt to a society that separated me from my true identity has exerted an array of negative outcomes I may never understand. Throughout it all, I've never given up on the hope that things would improve as I got older. It's been a very slow journey, however, and the events of 2020 were the equivalent of slamming into a brick wall. I witnessed instances of racism and social injustice that were similar to what I saw in person 30 years ago. And, the reactions I have seen from some of the people I thought I knew have been illuminating, in the most unfortunate way.

After placing my despair aside for a moment, I began to consider how these events have never really stopped. As a nation, we have just gotten better at hiding the underlying beliefs that cause these events and this has initiated a chain reaction. What could I do to make things better? How could I add value and make a positive, measurable change? In all honesty, taking to the streets and protesting did not seem like an option for me. With a corporate job that gave no allowances for getting arrested and a ridiculous array of financial obligations, I simply could not justify putting the future of my children at risk.

Researching this book has given me an even greater admiration for the people who have made themselves available to the public, facing threats and attaching their name to social justice causes. I have immeasurable respect for their braveness. Here in the Southern portion of the US, the racism can sometimes feel as palpable as the stifling humidity that plagues our area in the dog days of summer. There have been days when all I wanted to do was lock my entire family inside and not even go to the mailbox. I've never been able to understand why African Americans were so despised. The rabbit hole beckoned. Had my peers at work been hiding their disdain for me? Had they always disliked me and thought less of me? What about my neighbors? Where did it end? As a result, I decided to take back control, establish a business and treat people the way I would want to be treated. These were the catalysts for my decision to launch a diversity consulting business. Instead of leaving the corporate world behind, I opted to work from within as a consultant, in an effort to elicit a positive change. I was aware of the restrictions and lack of diversity that existed in corporate America, but as my research grew, I became aware that many marginalized minority groups existed. With the launch of my company, I'm hoping to improve workplace Diversity, Equity and Inclusion (DEI), thereby creating a healthy environment for any organization. The more experience I have gained in this area, the more I have realized that our work needs to be concentrated on our similarities and respecting our differences. There is more that unites us than many realize and I wanted to shed light on our commonalities. My main goal is to bring people together. Once we recognize that we are all humans with value and everybody has a story, the potential for grace and empathy increases exponentially. Working to level the playing field and stop pretending things are okay will lead to uncomfortable conversations, but these are essential to create a positive change.

Thank you to the warriors for equality and social justice, the survivors, and the historians who have recognized the value of documenting the good, the bad, and the ugly of our history.

Caroline

1

Understanding Diversity

*Diversity is about all of us and about us having to
figure out how to walk through this world together.*
—Jacqueline Woodson

The culture of the United States is multifaceted and DEI issues have had a significant impact on the individual throughout the history of the nation. It is essential to explore DEI practices in the workplace, since the majority of adult Americans interact in this environment in one way or another. The struggles of various groups to achieve equal rights were a hallmark of life in the 20th century. From the Winnipeg General Strike through the struggles for gender and LGBT equality, the 1900s were a century of change for many souls who–for various reasons–existed outside the traditionally-defined power structure of Western civilization.

Before determining whether it is possible to manage diversity, it is essential to first define what it is and identify the potential benefits. Diversity refers to the differences among people in the workforce and the needs that arise when people from differing backgrounds work together.

There are many obvious benefits to having a diverse workforce, including increased innovation and productivity. DEI also means valuing everyone's unique perspectives and seeking different ones when making decisions.

To help create an environment of inclusion and diversity, I launched a Diversity Consulting company, Bright Star Consulting. We offer DEI crisis consulting, education, and training. By providing assessments, consulting and certification programs on DEI practices in the workplace, we help our clients create a competitive advantage. I have accumulated detailed qualitative data as I have worked with companies to develop a more inclusive and diverse workplace. This data is in the form of stories about inclusion/exclusion, diversity and unconscious bias, which we share and discuss in our workplace training courses. From heartwarming to haunting, we've heard many stories as a result of our work.

The goal of this chapter is to provide a glimpse into the barriers faced by minorities. The contributions made to this book support the need to recognize the individual and evaluate all people by the same set of standards. Discussing experiences of diversity, equity and inclusion is critical because it has a significant impact on society and a massive impact on the economy. Workplace diversity is equally important. Diversity in the workplace is strongly linked to increased employee morale, higher levels of retention and reduced turnover. Awareness of this fact has the potential to encourage other organizations to adopt sound DEI practices.

What Is Diversity?

Diversity is the inclusion of a wide variety of people into a group or organization. Diversity is vital to the success of any organization and employers should understand the concepts it includes. Diversity relates to race, gender, age, sexual orientation, culture, religion, neurodiversity, employees with physical disabilities, and more.

Diversity, Equity & Inclusion Definitions

Types of Diversity

Cultural diversity

This aspect of DEI is related to ethnicity. It is commonly associated with the set of norms we get from the society we have been raised in, as well as the values embraced by our extended family. Of course, having a wide range of cultures in the workplace is typically more common in larger, multinational companies.

Racial Diversity

Though it may not be accurate, race has to do with someone's grouping based on bodily traits. The reason this definition may not be accurate is that the dominant scientific view is that race is a social construct and not biologically described, as previously imagined. Examples of races include Caucasian, African, Latino and Asian.

Religious Diversity

This sort of diversity pertains to the inclusion or exclusion of differing religions and/or non-secular beliefs in the workplace.

Age Diversity

Age diversity simply refers to having people of various ages and generations represented in the workplace. Some organizations may seek to only hire young or older workers; this would be what is known as age discrimination. Having people that would be termed as Millennials, GenZers, GenXers, etc., all within the same work environment, can allow for diverse viewpoints that drive the company forward.

Sex / Gender / Sexual Orientation

Sex and gender may be used in the traditional sense of male and female workers. It's not uncommon to hear company leaders express a desire to attain a 50/50 balance among employees who identify as male and employees who identify as female. This is commonly known as "gender balance." Understanding that the meaning of gender is constantly changing, however, "gender diversity" may be more appropriate because there is more than one variation regarding sexual orientation and/or gender.

Disability

There are varying types of disabilities and/or chronic health conditions, ranging from intellectual and mental to physical. Businesses often provide accommodations to help people with disabilities fit into the workplace. This would include putting in ramps for wheelchairs or providing intellectual health assistance. Some organizations also modify hiring techniques to ensure their processes are inclusive.

Additional Types of Diversity

In addition to the traits/characteristics protected by the Civil Rights Act, there are other forms of diversity, including:

- Socioeconomic background or class diversity
- Personality
- General worldview / opinions
- Education
- Life experiences

Of course, these traits are more intangible and difficult to identify than protected traits, however it's equally useful to take them into account within the context of commercial enterprise.

Call to Action

Business Case of Diversity

If every group member has the same background, attributes or views, the team might not be as innovative and successful as they need to be.

Homogeneity deprives teams of the kind of competition that brings innovation and development. Change starts with disposing of harmful biases when making employment decisions.

Benefits of Diversity

Diversity brings many perspectives to a company. This is positive for the growth of individual employees as well as the company as a whole. In study after study, it has been proven that companies with a diverse workforce create a diverse pool of knowledge. Having sound DEI policies in place helps to ensure legal compliance, establish a global customer base, increase the loyalty of employees, and assist in fulfilling the needs of existing customers.

Managing diversity is essential to the success of any organization. It is the responsibility of human resources (HR) to create a written policy. The goal is to ensure that all employees are treated equally, regardless of their gender, race, sexual orientation, neurodiversity, ethnicity, religion, etc.

It is also the responsibility of the HR team to ensure the company's diversity requirements and goals are communicated to leadership. The policy should be backed by the skills of the team, such as effective communication, treating each employee equally, and the collaboration/inclusion of diverse small groups within the larger group.

The leadership team must be trained to correctly implement the policy while creating a diverse and collaborative environment. Diversity is essential to the company's success; therefore management must be held accountable for its implementation.

Zero-Tolerance Policy

A zero-tolerance policy is designed to prevent objectionable behavior. These policies also outline the consequences for non-compliance. Each company is responsible for drafting its own policy and ensuring all the necessary elements are included. A few items include prohibiting the following: physical harm to others, discrimination, and sexual harassment. Supervisors and human resources play an integral role in monitoring noncompliant behavior. Some of the reporting methods include receiving complaints via hotlines or written reports. These should be followed by documented consequences for engaging in such behaviors, such as verbal warnings, termination, or legal action. Companies should be held accountable for the workplace environment. Implementing firm policies against workplace discrimination and harassment is essential. Most importantly, companies should encourage employees to report incidents and enforce punishment for non-compliance. Having a safe and healthy workplace also depends on the employee commitment as well—namely, understanding the policy and reporting issues.

True diversity promotes acceptance, respect and teamwork among employees. These are goals that should be promoted regardless of differences in race, age, gender, native language, political beliefs, religion, sexual orientation, or communication styles.

Diverse workplaces have been proven to excel in product and process innovation. The reason is simple. People from a variety of backgrounds working together can achieve more than those from one background. This is backed by reports showing companies that practice diversity and inclusion outperform non-diverse companies by an average of 15 percent. But as the workplace becomes increasingly diverse, businesses are faced with more issues. Recruitment professionals and the HR team should be aware of the various challenges associated with diversity. This aids in preventing and addressing any problems that may occur. With that in mind, the following is intended as a list of the most significant diversity issues in the workplace.

Acceptance and Respect

Respect between employees is a core value that helps a diverse workplace function smoothly. People from differing backgrounds who feel that they are free to share their ideas and beliefs at work can help to identify new ways to solve problems.

Prejudice and disrespect can lead to mistrust and a breakdown in communication, however. These factors and many others can make people feel like outsiders. It is easy to see why people are not going to be very productive if they do not feel their opinions and beliefs are going to be valued. Many other problems can also result from prejudice and disrespect. When these two factors are present, disagreements can quickly lead to anger and sometimes, violent interactions.

Employees can function at a higher level as a team and be more productive if they learn to accept and value their differences. Diversity training helps employees understand how their culture and values affect how they communicate, make decisions, and solve problems at work.

Accommodation of Beliefs

Having people with a wide variety of cultural, religious, and political beliefs can sometimes result in workplace issues and disagreements. Employees and business owners should never force their beliefs on others. In the vast majority of cases, it is essential to keep personal and ethnic beliefs separate from the work.

Ethnic and Cultural Differences

A report from the New York Times showed that five of the Fortune 500 companies in the United States have African-American CEOs. And a study from the University of Wisconsin found that people with names that sound like they are of African descent are 14 percent less likely to get a call back than people with names that sound like they are of European descent. It is unfortunate that ethnic and cultural differences can still amount to problems at work.

Bias, discrimination and unfair treatment should not be permissible within the modern workplace environment. Internal company policies should be put in place to prevent employees from maintaining cultural biases. Cultural sensitivity training and programs that teach people about diversity can help to solve this problem and bring people together.

Gender Equality

A recent poll found that 40 percent of both men and women think men are more likely to be hired than women. Two studies back this conclusion. One describes how men and women get promoted at different rates. This study (should we footnote or at least reference the specific name of the study?) showed that men are 30 percent more likely to receive a management position than women. In the second study, (same thing) it was found that male employees receive an average of 24 percent more compensation than female employees. Wages for women have historically been lower than those for their male counterparts. This unfair practice was made illegal when the Equal Pay Act was passed, however, an array of anecdotal evidence supports the thesis that males continue to receive higher levels of compensation for the same job. In the past few years, more women have started working and it has become more common for them to compete with men for the same jobs. Employers need to treat everyone the same when they hire, pay, provide opportunities and promotions.

Disabilities

Access for people with disabilities is often lacking, making it hard for many disabled employees to navigate the workplace. Some permissible accommodations include wheelchair ramps, places to sit, and elevators. Some people with disabilities also need service dogs. However, some organizations do not allow service dogs to be present in the workplace. Employers that want to maintain sound DEI policies should consider making accommodations to allow service dogs in the workplace.

An employer seeking to create effective DEI policies should learn about how to help people with physical or mental disabilities. Some companies have a "quiet room" where employees can go to calm down when they are feeling stressed. Creating a comfortable workplace environment for people with physical and mental disabilities could help the company attract a more diverse group of employees.

Generation Gaps

By 2025, approximately 75 percent of the workforce will be comprised of Millennials. A common stereotype relevant to younger generations is that they want to make sweeping changes, necessary or not. A common stereotype pertaining to older generations is they can be resistant to change. Of course, these factors can sometimes lead to conflict.

In bigger companies, it is not uncommon to see people of many different ages working together. When people in the same age group form cliques and social circles, however, others can feel excluded. To help the workplace function smoothly, a culture of open communication should be established to encourage coworkers of various ages to interact and collaborate with one another.

Language and Communication

Language and communication barriers exert a negative impact on the ability of a company to get things done. Multinational companies frequently hire people whose first language is not English. This can make it hard for supervisors and subordinates to talk to each other. When a company has a diverse workforce, there are real concerns over productivity losses and miscommunication.

To avoid these kinds of problems, it's best to hire people who speak more than one language. Recruiting employees from differing cultures and viewpoints can also have a positive impact. Doing so can result in a competitive advantage. In fact, it has been shown that companies with a diverse base of employees have a 35 percent higher level of performance than the national industry average.

2

History of the Diversity, Equity, and Inclusion Movement

*Inclusivity means not just "we're allowed to be
there," but we are valued. I've always said,
"Smart teams will do amazing things, but truly
diverse teams will do impossible things."*
—Claudia Brind-Woody

History of Cultural Diversity in the United States

Thousands of years before Europeans began crossing the Atlantic Ocean by ship and settling in huge numbers, the first immigrants arrived in North America and the land that would later become the United States. Of course, the ancestors of the Native Americans were already in North America, as they had used a narrow land bridge to cross over from Asia approximately 20,000 years ago, during the last Ice Age.

The concept of diversity is nothing new. In fact, American culture has always been diverse. Native American tribes inhabited North America thousands of years before the first white settlers. Colonists from Europe arrived in waves, building communities and leaving their own imprint. Africans brought over through the slave trade hundreds of years ago created a rich culture that would eventually be assimilated into mainstream American culture. Millions of immigrants have also contributed to this colorful patchwork. By and large, the US is an amalgam of peoples from around the world, and it has been since the very beginning.

Viewed through the lens of history, it is easy to see how cultural diversity has shaped the United States and its citizens. The history of cultural diversity in the US has been dominated by extended periods of racial intolerance, when people were persecuted for their differences. It is important to note that there have been important legal moves forward to support equality. Unfortunately, many of these steps in the right direction have been followed by giant steps backward. The periods of tolerance when diverse groups of people could live together without much conflict have been relatively brief. There are a number of potential explanations for why these periods have evaporated, though it is difficult to argue against the idea that many have maintained beliefs that support the division in our country and racial intolerance.

The History of Indigenous People in the United States

A description of the history of diversity in the United States would be incomplete without mentioning the Native Americans. The Americas were their home for generations, long before Christopher Columbus made his 'discovery.' As more explorers and immigrants tried to settle on the land that was inhabited by indigenous people, their reactions ranged from peace and cooperation to anger, conflict and war.

By the end of the 19th century, Native American populations were smaller. They were confined to small reservations and suffered unspeakable cruelties. This was partially due to the fact they sided with the French in many battles during the French and Indian War and because Andrew Jackson's Indian Removal Act forced them to leave their homes.

Indigenous People Timeline

Christopher Columbus arrived on a Caribbean Island in 1492 after traveling for three months. Initially, he thought he was in the East Indies, so he called the native people he met "Indians." On his first day, he advised his crew to take six of them as servants.

In April 1513, the Spanish explorer Juan Ponce de León landed in Florida on the continent of North America and met the native people there.

In February of 1521, Ponce de León left San Juan to start a new settlement in Florida. Months after he landed, the local native people attacked and killed him.

Hernando de Soto, a Spanish explorer and conqueror, landed in Florida in May 1539 to take control of the area. He toured the South searching for gold, with the help of Native Americans who were taken prisoner along the way.

In October of 1540, de Soto and the Spaniards traveled to Alabama to meet with resupply vessels. After demanding women and servants from Chief Tuskaloosa, who refused, de Soto and his soldiers took him hostage and were subsequently ambushed by his tribe. The Spaniards killed around 2,000 to 4,000 Native Americans that day in the battle that followed, making it one of the bloodiest in the nation's history.

Pocahontas is born in 1595 to Chief Powhatan. Captain John Smith is taken from the Jamestown colony by Pocahontas' brother in 1607. Smith would later write that Pocahontas saved him when Chief Powhatan tried to hurt him. Historians disagree about what might have happened.

During the first Anglo-Powhatan War, Pocahontas is taken by Captain Samuel Argall in 1613. During her time in captivity, she learned English, became a Christian and took the name "Rebecca."

The Jamestown colony is nearly destroyed by the Powhatan Confederacy in 1622.

In 1680, a group of Native Pueblo people in New Mexico rose up against Spanish rule.

The French and Indian War started in 1754, pitting the French and Native Americans against English settlements in the north.

On May 15, 1756, the British and the French started the Seven Years' War. The French were helped by Native American alliances.

The Battle of Detroit began on May 7, 1763; with Chief Pontiac of the Ottawa tribe led Native American forces against the British. In response, on July 31, the British attacked Pontiac's warriors in Detroit. This is known as the Battle of Bloody Run. Pontiac and his group were able to fight them off, but there were losses on both sides.

In 1785, the Treaty of Hopewell was signed in Georgia. It protected Native Americans from the Cherokee tribe and divided up their land.

Sacagawea was born in 1788 or 1789.

The Treaty of Holston was signed in 1791, resulting in the Cherokee giving up all their land outside of the borders that had been previously defined.

The Battle of Fallen Timbers started on August 20, 1794. It was the last major conflict between Native Americans and the United States over northwest territories after the Revolutionary War. The US had a decisive victory.

Native American Sacagawea met Meriwether Lewis and William Clark on November 2, 1804, when they were exploring the area of the Louisiana Purchase. Sacagawea was six months pregnant at the time. The explorers immediately recognized her gifts as a translator.

On April 7, 1805, Sacagawea, her baby and her husband Toussaint Charbonneau went on the trip with Lewis and Clark.

In November 1811, Chief Tecumseh and his younger brother Lalawethika were attacked by US troops. Their town was destroyed at the point where the Tippecanoe and Wabash rivers meet.

On June 18, 1812, President James Madison signed a declaration of war against Britain. This started the war between US forces and the British, French, and Native Americans over independence and territory expansion.

In the Battle of Horseshoe Bend, which took place on March 27, 1814,

Andrew Jackson, US troops and Native American allies attacked Creek Indians who were against American expansion and encroachment on their land. After losing, the Creeks gave up more than 20 million acres of land. President Andrew Jackson signed the Indian Removal Act on March 28, 1830. This law gave Native American tribes pieces of land west of the Mississippi River in exchange for land that was taken from them.

As part of the Indian removal process, the last of the Creek people left their land for Oklahoma in 1836. More than 3,500 of the 15,000 Creeks who left for Oklahoma did not make it.

In 1838, only 2,000 Cherokees had left their land in Georgia to cross the Mississippi River. President Martin Van Buren asked General Winfield Scott and 7,000 troops to speed up the process by holding the Cherokees at gunpoint and marching them 1,200 miles. Because of the trip, more than 5,000 Cherokee people died. This awful stain on the nation's history has been called the Trail of Tears, as a result of the hardships and deaths that happened to Native American tribes along the way.

Congress passed the Indian Appropriations Act in 1851, which set up the system of Indian reservations. Native Americans are restricted to their reserves and prohibited from traveling without official approval.

In October 1860, a group of Apaches attacked and kidnapped a white American. The US military wrongly blamed Cochise, the leader of the Chiricahua Apache tribe, for this crime. For the next ten years, Cochise and the Apache completed more raids on white Americans.

The Sand Creek Massacre occurred on November 29, 1864, when 650 volunteers from Colorado attacked Cheyenne and Arapaho camps along Sand Creek. They killed and mutilated more than 150 Native Americans.

On November 27, 1868, General George Armstrong Custer led an early morning raid on the Cheyenne hamlet where he was staying, killing more than a hundred people. The casualties included women and children, as well as Chief Black Kettle.

General Custer met Crazy Horse for the first time in 1873.

When gold was found in the Black Hills of South Dakota in 1874, US troops broke a treaty and invaded the area.

On June 25, 1876, Lieutenant Colonel George Custer's troops fought Lakota Sioux and Cheyenne warriors led by Crazy Horse and Sitting Bull at the Battle of Little Bighorn, in what would become known as "Custer's Last Stand." Custer and his soldiers lost the battle and were killed, which increased the division between whites and Native Americans.

The first students started going to Carlisle Indian Industrial School in Pennsylvania on October 6, 1879. It was the first boarding school outside of a reservation. The school, which was started by Civil War veteran Richard Henry Pratt, was meant to help Native American students fit in with the rest of society.

First Hand account of Indigenous Peoples Assimilation Schools

"Kill the Indian in him so that the man can live."
- Richard Henry Pratt

These were the words that US Cavalry Captain Richard Henry Pratt used to open the first boarding school in Carlisle, Pennsylvania. Sadly, this quote has come to represent the harshness of the boarding school system over the years.

In the late 19th century, the US government forced tens of thousands of Native American children into boarding schools for "assimilation." The history of this forced assimilation is not at all clear. In 2017, the US Army started digging up the graves of three Northern Arapaho children who had died at Pratt's Carlisle Indian Industrial School in the 1880s. The children' names were Little Chief, Horse, and Little Plume. They were told by school officials they would not be allowed to use those names.

Yufna Soldier Wolf of the Northern Arapaho, in the middle, with tribal elders Mark Soldier Wolf and Crawford White Sr., holds pictures of Little Plume, Horse, and Little Chief. Around 135 years ago, three Arapaho children died while going to school in Pennsylvania. They were buried at the Carlisle Indian School, which was run by the government.

Native People's School.jpg

The students at Carlisle and the other schools like it that the government had opened, around 150 in total, were at risk of getting diseases like tuberculosis and the flu, which was life-threatening at the time. The Northern Arapaho boys and approximately 200 other children were buried in the same cemetery between 1879 and 1918, when Carlisle was in operation.

The efforts put forth by the US to expel, exterminate and integrate indigenous people go back for many years. Carlisle and the other boarding schools are just a small example of the work that has been done to minimize indigenous populations. With the Indian Removal Act of 1830, the US forced Native Americans to move west of the Mississippi River so the country could grow. In only a few short decades, however, the US worried there would not be enough room for its burgeoning population.

The Minnesota Historical Society says, "As the number of white people in the United States grew and people moved west toward the Mississippi in the late 1800s, there was more pressure on the people who had just moved there to give up some of their new land." Since there was no more Western land to move them to, the US decided to eliminate indigenous people through assimilation. In 1885, Hiram Price, the Commissioner of Indian Affairs, said, "It is cheaper to educate them than to fight them."

The Carlisle Indian School

As part of the Federal push for assimilation, Native American children in boarding schools were forbidden from using their own languages or given names. They were also not allowed to practice their religion or culture. These children were given new Anglo-American names, clothes, and haircuts. They were also told their way of life was inferior to that of white people and that it should be forgotten.

The schools had a terrible effect on Native American cultures, but luckily, the goal of eradicating their way of life did not succeed. Later, the Navajo Code Talkers who helped the US win World War II would think about how strange it was that they were forced to become more like everyone else.

The following statement from the National Museum of the American Indian illustrates this idea: "As adults, [the Code Talkers] found it strange that the same government that had tried to take away their languages in schools then gave them a key role in speaking their languages in the military."

According to Philly.com, the Northern Arapaho of Wyoming, the

Rosebud Sioux of South Dakota and the native people of Alaska are all trying to get the remains of children from Carlisle. But if the search results from the Northern Arapaho are any indication, this may be very difficult.

At the family graveyard on the Wind River Reservation in Wyoming near Riverton, Yufna Soldier Wolf wipes tears as she pays her respects to her great-grandfather, Chief Sharp Nose of the Northern Arapaho Tribe.

AP Photo by Dan Cepeda/The Casper Star-Tribune

The Army sent the bodies of Little Chief and Horse back to their families on the Wind River Reservation on August 14, 2017. On August 18, 2017, the Northern Arapaho buried them. The body of Little Plume, on the other hand, was not returned because no one could find him. Archaeologists found the bones of two other people in what they thought to be the coffin of Little Plume. The bones could not have belonged to Little Plume because they were too old.

Researchers do not know who those two people were or where Little Plume could be, and the Northern Arapaho have not provided an indication on whether they will continue looking for him. The Army has reburied the two people found in Little Plume's coffin, but he is still one of Carlisle's many missing children.

Timeline of the Indigenous People's Integration of Diversity

On February 8, 1887, President Grover Cleveland signed the Dawes Act. This law allowed the president to allocate land in reservations to different people.

On December 15, 1890, Sitting Bull was killed in Grand River, South Dakota, during a fight with Indian police.

On December 29, 1890, armed forces from the US surrounded a group of ghost dancers led by Chief Big Foot near Wounded Knee Creek in South Dakota. The dancers were told to give up their weapons. During the Wounded Knee massacre, about 150 Native Americans and 25 US cavalry soldiers died.

Charles Curtis was the first Native American to become a US Senator on January 29, 1907.

During WWI in the Meuse-Argonne Offensive on the Western Front in September 1918, Choctaw soldiers used their native language to send secret messages to their fellow soldiers. The Choctaw Telephone Squad gave the Allies a significant advantage over the Germans.

On June 2, 1924, the US Congress passed the Indian Citizenship Act, making all Native Americans born within the country's borders citizens. In the past, citizenship was limited based on how much Native American ancestry a person had, whether they were a veteran, a woman, or married to a US citizen.

Read more: 20 Rare Photos of Native American
(??) Life at the Turn of the Century

Charles Curtis became the first Native American Vice President of the United States on March 4, 1929. He worked for President Herbert Hoover.

During World War II, members of the Navajo nation came up with a code to send messages for the US military. Hundreds of code talkers from different Native American tribes eventually served the nation in the US Marines.

President Lyndon B. Johnson signed the Indian Civil Rights Act into law on April 11, 1968. This gave Native American tribes many of the rights in the Bill of Rights.

On March 15, 2021, Representative Deb Haaland of New Mexico is confirmed as Secretary of the Interior. She is the first Native American to lead a cabinet agency. Haaland wrote on Twitter after her confirmation that, "Growing up in my mother's Pueblo home made me tough. I'll fight hard for all of us, our planet, and our protected land."

As soon as Europeans landed on American shores, the frontier became a place where conflict and violence were common. The frontier, of course, was the wilder natural area beyond the white man's civilization. For a variety of reasons, including a desire for more land, the US government authorized more than 1,500 wars, attacks and raids on Native Americans, more than any other country in the world. By the end of the Indian Wars in the late 1800s, there were only about 238,000 Native Americans left. This represented a substantial decline from the approximately five to 15 million people who lived in North America when Columbus arrived in 1492.

The hunger for Native American land and its natural resources were partially due to the fact that most of the settlers could not inherit land in Europe. Also, during the American Revolution and the War of 1812, the Native Americans helped the British. This made Americans even more angry and suspicious of them.

Indigenous people were also fundamentally different because their skin was dark. Their languages sounded much different from the settlers. And, it is worth pointing out that many of the white men could not understand their ideas about the world or their spiritual beliefs. This made the white settlers fear that one of their loved ones could become the next Mary Campbell, who was taken captive as a child by Native Americans during the French and Indian War. Fueling racial hatred and describing Native Americans as savages made it easier to justify killing them in the name of civilization and Christianity.

Acts of genocide against Native Americans are
shown above, the Gnadenhutten Massacre.

In 1782, a group of Pennsylvania militiamen killed 96 Native Americans from Delaware who had become Christians. This showed

the growing disrespect for native people. Captain David Williamson told the converted Delawares, who had been blamed for attacks on white settlements, to go to the cooper shop two at a time. There, militiamen beat them to death with wooden mallets and hatchets.

Ironically, the Delawares were the first Native Americans to capture a white settler and the first to sign a US-Indian treaty four years earlier. This treaty set the standard for the next 100 years, when 374 more treaties were signed. Many of these agreements used the phrase "peace and friendship," and 229 of them led to tribal lands being given to the United States, which was growing quickly at the time. Many treaties were made to set up trade between the US and the Indians. The intent was to get rid of the British and their goods, especially the guns they gave to the Native Americans.

In the early 1800s, the rise of the charismatic Shawnee war leader Tecumseh and his brother, who was known as the Prophet, convinced Native Americans of different tribes that it was in their best interest to stop fighting among themselves and work together to protect their mutual interests. In 1811, Indiana Territorial Governor and future President William Henry Harrison attacked and burned Prophetstown, the Native Americans' capital on the Tippecanoe River, while Tecumseh was away trying to recruit more warriors from the Choctaws. This made the Shawnee leader want to attack again. This time, he was able to get the British to join his warriors in fighting against the Americans. In 1813, when Tecumseh was defeated at the Battle of the Thames and died, the Ohio frontier became "safe" for settlers, for a while.

In the South, the War of 1812 led to the Creek War of 1813–1814, also known as the Red Stick War. The war was between different groups of Creek Indians. It also involved US militias, as well as the British and Spanish, who helped the Native Americans keep the Americans from getting in the way of their interests. General Andrew Jackson responded to early Creek victories by sending 2,500 men, mostly from the Tennessee militia, to fight back in early November 1814. Jackson and his men killed 186 Creeks at Tallushatchee to get back at the Creeks for killing people at Fort Mims. Davy Crockett said, "We shot them like dogs!"

Desperate, the women killed their children so they wouldn't have to see the soldiers kill them. Andrew Jackson, the future president, grabbed a baby from a woman who was about to kill her child. Later, he gave the baby Native American to his wife, Rachel, to raise as their own.

Jackson won the Red Stick War at Horseshoe Bend in a decisive battle. In the next treaty, the Creek had to give the United States more than 21 million acres of land.

America's Cultural Diversity Growth through Immigration

US Immigration before 1965

During the colonial era, the first half of the 19th century, and from the 1880s to 1920, many people came to the United States. People came to America in search of better jobs and a better life.

People have always thought of the United States as a country of immigrants. Over time, the feelings that earlier immigrants have had about newer immigrants have vacillated between inclusion and exclusion. The first people to come to North America and the land that would become the United States did so thousands of years before Europeans began settling in large numbers. During the last Ice Age, about 20,000 years ago, the first Americans crossed a narrow strip of land that connected Asia to North America. By the start of the 1600s, there were many European communities along the East Coast. The Spanish lived in Florida, the British in New England and Virginia, the Dutch in New York, and the Swedes in Delaware. Some people came for religious freedom, like the Pilgrims and the Puritans. Many were in search of more money. The hundreds of thousands of Africans who were brought to America as slaves, of course, did not want to be there. The following events have occurred since the United States was founded, changing the history of immigration.

Timeline: History of Immigration in the United States

Thomas Paine put out a pamphlet called "Common Sense" in January 1776. It argued for American independence. Most colonists at the time thought of themselves as British, but Paine argued for a new American identity. He wrote that, "Europe, not England, is where America came from. Persecuted supporters of civil and religious freedom from all over Europe have found refuge in this new world."

In March 1790, Congress made the first law about who could be a citizen of the United States. The Naturalization Act of 1790 said that any free white person who has lived in the United States for at least two years and has "good character" can apply to become a citizen. Without citizenship, nonwhite residents would not be allowed to vote, own property or testify in court, among other fundamental constitutional rights.

In August 1790, the first census of the United States was taken. The English are the largest group, with 3.9 million people. However, nearly one in five Americans was of African descent.

Waves of Irish Immigrants

After the War of 1812, the US and Britain made peace again, in 1815. The number of people coming to the United States from Western Europe went from a trickle to a flood. This changed the way people live in the United States. This first big wave of people coming to the United States lasted until the Civil War.

Between 1820 and 1860, about a third of all people who came to the United States were Irish, most of them Catholic. Approximately five million Germans also moved to the US, mainly settling in the Midwest, where they bought farms and moved to cities like Milwaukee, St. Louis, and Cincinnati.

In response to the influx of people immigrating to the US, Congress passed the Steerage Act of 1819. Major port cities such as New York, Boston, Philadelphia and Charleston were being overrun by immigrants. Many were arriving sick or dead, due to the long, arduous journey across the Atlantic. The act required ships arriving in the country to be in better shape. It also required ship captains to give demographic information about their passengers. This is the first time the government kept track of the ethnic backgrounds of people who came to the United States.

In 1849, the first anti-immigrant political party was formed in the United States. It is a reaction to the growing number of German and Irish people moving to the United States.

After the Civil War ended in 1875, some states made laws about immigration. Finally, in 1875, the Supreme Court said that creating and enforcing immigration laws was the responsibility of the Federal Government.

Chinese Exclusion Act

In 1880, a second wave of immigrants came to the US, just as the country was becoming more industrialized. From 1880 to 1920, more than 20 million people relocated to the United States. Most of them were from Southern, Eastern and Central Europe. Four million

Italians and two million Jews were among them. Many of them moved to big cities in the US, where they worked in factories. The Chinese Exclusion Act was passed in 1882, making it illegal for Chinese people to come to the US. Since the 1850s, many Chinese workers had come to America to find jobs. They worked in gold mines and clothing factories. They also built railroads and farmed. As Chinese workers got ahead in America, negative perceptions about them grew. Although Chinese immigrants only made up around 0.002 percent of the US population, white workers blamed low wages on them. The 1882 Act was the first time in U.S. history that significant restrictions were placed on specific immigrant groups.

1800s Asian immigrants

Around the middle of the 1800s, the first large group of Asian immigrants came to the United States. Since then, Asian Americans have played an important role in US history, but they have also had to deal with discrimination and exclusion. More than 20 million Asian Americans in the United States hail from over 20 countries in Asia and India, according to the Pew Research Center. Most Asian Americans today are Chinese, Indian, Filipino, Vietnamese, Korean, or Japanese.

In 1891, the Immigration Act added more people to the list of those who were not allowed to relocate to the United States. It said that polygamists, people convicted of certain crimes and people who were sick or had diseases were barred from entry. The Act also set up a Federal Office of Immigration to coordinate enforcement activities and a corps of immigration inspectors to work at major ports of entry.

In January 1892, Ellis Island opened in New York Harbor as the first immigration station in the United States. Annie Moore, an Irish teen from County Cork, was the first person to be processed as an immigrant. Between 1892 and 1954, more than 12 million people came to the United States through Ellis Island.

Ellis Island is a historically significant landmark that opened in 1892 and operated as an immigration station for more than 60 years, until its doors were finally closed in 1954. Ellis Island is an expanse of land that stretches between New York and New Jersey at the end of the Hudson River. Between 1892 and 1954, more than 12 million immigrants came to the United States through Ellis Island. This made the American population more diverse than it had been before.

In the late 19th century and early 20th century, many people from Northern and Western Europe came to the United States on ships that were overcrowded. They left Europe to get away from hunger and religious discrimination, to buy farmland, and live the American dream. On April 17, 1907, nearly 12,000 people came to the United States through Ellis Island.

In 1907, 1.3 million people came
to the US, a record high.

In February 1907, the United States and Japan signed the Gentlemen's Agreement. At the time, people in California were afraid that more Japanese workers would take jobs from white farmers and drive down wages. As a result, Japan agreed that only certain types of businessmen and professionals would be allowed to immigrate to the US. In return, President Theodore Roosevelt told San Francisco to stop putting Japanese students in separate schools from white students.

The Chinese Exclusion Era was from 1920 to 1940.

Angel Island Immigration Station

From 1910 to 1940, the Angel Island Immigration Station in San Francisco Bay was the central entry point for immigration on the West Coast of the United States. Because of the Chinese Exclusion Act of 1882 and other unfair immigration laws, many people from China and other Asian countries were held there for long periods.

In the wake of the Gold Rush, many people from China came to the United States. Some worked as miners, others worked on farms, some worked in textile factories, others on the transcontinental railroad. At the time, the Federal government did not exert much control over immigration. Instead, the states were left to decide. As the number of immigrants from Europe and Asia grew, however, this necessitated the Federal government stepping in to enact regulations. This was especially true after a bad economy in the 1870s caused many Americans to blame immigrant workers for their problems.

At the time, the eugenics movement, which is essentially the study of how to plan for reproduction in a human population to increase the prevalence of heritable characteristics regarded as desirable, was gaining strength. Many worried about other races or ethnicities "contaminating" the white race. Chinese immigrants were seen as a more significant threat than those from Ireland or Germany. In 1875, Congress passed the Page Act, which stopped Chinese, Japanese, and other Asian workers who were forced to come to the US from entering. It also stopped Asian women who were brought to the US to work as prostitutes from entering.

New Restrictions Implemented at the Start of WWI

On the eve of World War I, in 1917, xenophobia reached a new peak. The Immigration Act of 1917 made it a requirement for immigrants to be able to read and write. It also stopped people from most Asian countries from entering the US.

In May of 1924, the Immigration Act enacted a quota system, limiting the number of people from various countries who can come to the United States each year. Under this new quota system, immigration visas were given to two percent of the total number of people from each country that lived in the US in 1890. The law was designed to encourage immigration from countries in Northern and Western Europe. Of all the visas that were provided, 70 percent went to just three countries: Great Britain, Ireland, and Germany. The number of immigrants hailing from Southern, Central, and Eastern Europe were relatively low. The Act barred immigrants from everywhere in Asia except for the Philippines, which was an American colony at the time.

One outcome that resulted from the law of 1924 was that more people came to the US illegally. The US Border Patrol was established to stop immigrants from illegally crossing the borders with Mexico and Canada. Many of the first people to cross the border illegally were from China and other Asian countries. It is understandable given the fact the law prohibited them from legal entry into the country.

Mexicans Fill Labor Shortages During WWII

Because of a lack of workers during World War II, the US and Mexico created the Bracero Program in 1942, allowing Mexican farm workers to come to the US for short periods. The program ran through 1964.

In 1948, the US passed its first refugee and resettlement law in an effort to deal with the many Europeans who wanted to settle in the US permanently after World War II.

The McCarran-Walter Act of 1952 made it permissible for Asian immigrants to come to the United States.

After a failed uprising against the Soviets in 1956 and 1957, the US provided entry for around 38,000 Hungarians. They were some of the first people to flee the Cold War. The US took in more than three million refugees during the Cold War.

Between 1960 and 1962, about 14,000 unaccompanied children left Cuba under Fidel Castro and came to the United States as part of Operation Peter Pan, a secret anti-Communism program.

Quota System Ends

In 1965, the Immigration and Nationality Act changed how people immigrated to the United States. The Act eliminated the national origin quotas that were put in place in the 1920s. It also provided more jobs to people of some races and cultures than others.

A seven-category preference system was implemented to replace the quota system. The system gave priority to family reunification and skilled immigrants. When President Lyndon B. Johnson signed the new bill, he said the old immigration system was "un-American" and the new bill would fix a "cruel and lasting wrong" in the way the United States ran its government.

In the next five years, more than four times as many people moved to the United States from Vietnam, Cambodia and other war-torn parts of Asia. Family reunification became a big reason why people immigrated to the US.

During the Mariel boatlift, which took place from April to October of 1980, around 125,000 Cuban refugees made a dangerous sea crossing in overcrowded boats to get to the coast of Florida. They were looking for political asylum.

Amnesty to Illegal Immigrants

In 1986, President Ronald Reagan signed the Simpson-Mazzoli Act into law. The law gave amnesty to more than three million illegal immigrants living in the US.

In 2001, Senators Dick Durbin (D-Ill.) and Orrin Hatch (R-Utah) introduced the first Development, Relief and Education of Alien Minors (DREAM) Act to create a path to legal status for certain illegal immigrants. Dreamers are undocumented immigrants who were brought to the United States unlawfully by their parents when they were children. The bill is yet to pass.

The Deferred Action for Childhood Arrivals (DACA) program was signed into law by President Obama in 2012, providing temporary protection from deportation for some Dreamers but not a path to citizenship.

In 2017, President Trump signed two executive orders with the same title—"Protecting the Nation from Foreign Terrorist Entry into the United States"—to restrict travel and immigration from six mostly Muslim nations (Chad, Iran, Libya, Syria, Yemen, and Somalia), as well as North Korea and Venezuela. State and federal courts are looking into both of these travel bans.

After April of 2018, the restrictions on traveling to Chad expired. In June of 2018, a third version of the ban on the other seven countries was upheld by the US Supreme Court.

Implications of United States Immigration Over Time

On April 17, 1907, thousands of immigrants went through the registry room at Ellis Island, which was about the size of two high school basketball courts. By the end of the day, they had processed 11,747 immigrants the most ever in a single day. By the end of the year, over a million more immigrants would join them, starting new lives as Americans. Now, more than 110 years later, millions of people in the United States can say they are their children or grandchildren.

The goals of the people who came to America in 1907 seem clear. They wanted to plant a flag, realize the American Dream, and help their children and grandchildren become proud, upstanding citizens of the United States. Things were not always easy or straight-forward, however. Immigration was a very controversial topic back then, just as it is now. In 1907, people who wanted to live in the US didn't need much. There were no visas or papers, and the portion of immigrants in the US population had grown from less than 10 percent to more than 14 percent, which is about the same as today. People against immigration asked pointed questions about how new immigrants would fit into America. They also said immigrants would take jobs from Americans and spread xenophobia.

We now know those fears about people not fitting in were unfounded. The people who had a problem with immigrants in 1907 were Americans. Yet the same myths and fears surrounding immigration kept going around.

Critics of immigration said that immigrants today are less likely to adapt and succeed than immigrants in the past, even those who came in 1907.

But how were the people who immigrated in 1907 different from the immigrants of 2017? We can answer some of these questions because of the 1910 Census. Data from the 1910 Census and the 2017 American Community Survey show that:

- Modern immigrants speak more English. More than 83 percent of the immigrants who came to the United States in 2017 spoke some English or spoke it well. Nearly half of the people who came to America in 1907 did not speak any English at all.
- Immigrants today are more skilled than those who came in 1907. For example, in 1907, only 1.3 percent of immigrants had professional, skilled, or technical jobs, such as lawyers and engineers. In 2017, however, more than 34 percent of immigrants were classified as skilled workers.
- There is more variety among modern immigrants. For example, in 1907, almost 9 out of 10 people who came to the United States were from Europe. In 2017, however, immigrants were from nations such as China, Brazil and India. In fact, in 2017, none of the top 10 countries of origin were in Europe.
- Today, there are about the same number of immigrants in each state. More than half of the people who came to the United States in 1907 chose to live in New York, New Jersey, Pennsylvania, and Illinois. In 2017, immigrants were most likely to live in the western and southern states, especially California, Texas, and Florida. However, immigrants moved to every state in 2017.

The economy has changed a lot in the past 110 years, but immigrants have always been a big part of what drives the US economy, as they have always worked in key sectors. In 1907, agriculture, small mills, and factories—industries that require a lot of manual labor—were still the economy's main drivers. Today, almost 80 percent of the US economy is driven by the services sector, which includes retail and wholesale trade, entertainment, legal and professional services. Both native-born Americans and immigrants have been making the transition from labor-intensive positions to those requiring higher levels of education and training. The percent of immigrants working in professional and technical occupations increased from just over one percent in 1907 to over 34 percent in 2017.

Ellis Island Now 2020 (U.S. Census, 2017)

3

Diversity in the 21st Century

*Progress is possible, but it is fragile—and across our
country, the battles for our most basic civil rights rage on.*
—Stacey Abrams

Diversity is a term that can be used in many contexts. Although
diversity can be used to refer to a mixture of different races, ethnicities,
genders, sexual orientations, and ages, it is more commonly used to
describe the mixing of races and ethnicities. In many cases, diversity
has traditionally been viewed as something that only matters as far as
the importance of being politically correct. More importantly for many
business leaders and corporate stakeholders, however, is the fact that
diversity is a critical success factor in the modern economy.

Many of us remember learning about Rosie the Riveter, a marketing
concept that was created during World War II in an effort to encourage
more women to join the workforce. It was a response to the fact that the
vast majority of male employees had left the country to join the war effort.
Showing tenacity, resolve and determination, women stepped up to fill

many roles in the workplace. The conflict showed that women were just as capable at performing most of the same job functions as men, and many believe the war effort would not have been unsuccessful without them. When the war was over, however, women were expected to return to the home. Although the post-war era has often been depicted as a golden age for the traditional nuclear family, there was a significant backlash against this idea as many women fought for their right to continue working.

Over the last two decades, female participation in the US workforce has steadily increased. The percentage of employed women reached an all-time high in 1999, when 60 percent of women were in the workforce. The figure has remained around 57 percent since then.

By the 2010s, women had made significant strides in the workplace. This may have led many employers to believe that gender diversity was no longer a concern. When Uber reported several instances of sexual harassment in 2017, however, many began to question whether more work needed to be done to promote equality and respect in the workplace.

In the coming years, the concept of neurodiversity will gain a more prominent role in diversity discussions. The evolving concept of neurodiversity refers to the integration of people with different ways of thinking. Similar to other aspects of diversity, employers and recruiters will seek to integrate people with these traits into the workforce to enhance innovation and boost productivity. It is also likely that employers will become more accepting of their employees who occupy the neurodiversity portion of the spectrum. Thus, the ability to think outside the box will become a more attractive skill than it already is.

The debate surrounding diversity in the workplace has continued since the end of WWII, with changing legislation and court rulings affecting the rights of women, the disabled and workers from different ethnicities, cultures, sexual orientations and religions. The workplace of the future will likely be much more diverse than it was in the past. The push for diversity has made substantial progress in the last several decades, but the fight for equity and inclusion faces a number of ongoing challenges.

Diversity means a mixture of different things. The term refers to people of different backgrounds, ages, beliefs, ethnicities, sexual orientations and cultures. In the United States today, however, diversity is often thought of as solely a racial idea. Diversity is an essential component of the American experience. Americans of all ages, races and faiths contribute to diversity in culture and traditions. Diversity education allows people to understand the impact individuals may have on one another by fostering mutual respect for their differences.

Diversity training is distinct from diversity education, as it is focused the awareness of employees, their attitudes, knowledge base and skills. Diversity education combines diversity best practices to increase cultural diversity and belonging. Both are offered to small- and medium-size businesses by the governing body of the European Union (EU). This is provided in an effort to promote cultural diversity. By providing diversity training to businesses, the EU is hoping to increase the international/ cultural awareness of firms across the region.

Many governments and private entities such as corporations and universities are using diversity education to address historical discrimination. In Australia, these efforts are focused on ending discrimination against Aboriginal people. In Asia, diversity initiatives are concentrated on increasing productivity in companies with multinational employees. South Africa is adopting diversity concepts to adjust to the end of apartheid. In the US, diversity education was initially offered in response to the civil rights movement. However, the implementation of diversity education has continued as a result of the many proven benefits it provides.

Diversity in the United States

Over the years, diversity training developed in response to the fact that community, military, and educational institutions recognized there was a need to create a more tolerant workforce. Many businesses began using diversity training in the late 1980s and throughout the 1990s to protect against litigation and settle civil rights lawsuits. Diversity training, which has shifted functions and uses throughout the decades, is now considered an organizational necessity to provide all employees with equal access, regardless of gender, race, or religion. Diversity education has evolved over time as both a tool for achieving organizational goals and as part of an ethical obligation to treat employees fairly. The changing roles that diversity training efforts have played within organizations have caused many assumptions and beliefs about its value to evolve over time.

Diversity education began as a reaction to the civil rights movement and violent demonstrations by activists determined to make White Americans aware that Black citizens would no longer remain silent about their treatment. However, many activists realized that pursuing social stability would be a more effective means of achieving equality. This is a partial explanation for why diversity education and training initiatives have been developed in an effort to increase sensitivity and raise awareness about racial differences.

In the 1960s, the use of encounter groups as a diversity education platform became widespread. The goal behind creating encounter groups was to create an environment where people of differing racial backgrounds would be comfortable discussing sensitive issues. For example, an encounter group was held on an army base as part of a military experiment. The bar for calling the event a success was low. Facilitators viewed the event as successful after one white American admitted to having racist beliefs and shed a few tears over racial discrimination.

To illuminate the differences between the perspectives concerning race relations, facilitators brought in white participants who did not think they had racist beliefs. The decision to use facilitators that were both Black and White was essential for achieving cross-cultural collaboration in this diversity training program. The facilitators were typically men. In most cases, the White facilitator received higher marks if he was able to openly show emotions about his journey in discovering his racist personal beliefs. The facilitators believed they were working toward equality in a world that had historically oppressed those with less social, political and economic power. It was common for them to confront White Americans who made excuses for their racism or denied it altogether; their goal was to increase the sensitivity of White Americans to the effects of racial inequities.

During these intensive encounters, White participants in sensitivity training were affected in three distinct ways. One group became more aware of the barriers to racial harmony and was inspired to work toward overcoming those barriers. Another group resisted this awareness, gaining confidence in their belief that racial injustice did not exist or was a rare occurrence. Finally, a third group responded by becoming "fanatics" about racial equality; they began openly advocating against racism after sensitivity training.

According to research by H. R. Day, the Defense Department Race Relations Institute shortened its diversity training program in response to negative evaluations and mounting criticism. A decision was also made to curtail the use of "hot seat" techniques during diversity training sessions. Corporations ended the use of extreme diversity training methods when the Federal government started limiting affirmative action laws.

The notion of gender diversity education became a topic of discussion in the 1970s and 1980s, but the diversity education movement did not really expand to include other identity groups until the 1990s.

Through education and training efforts, various groups started to gain an insight into how people with disabilities, differing cultural backgrounds, religious beliefs and sexual orientations see the world. Diversity education started to appear in the in the United States in the 1970s. Prior to the 1990s, however, diversity efforts were primarily focused on barriers to inclusion for racial minorities. A shift in diversity education took place in the US in the 1990s, emphasizing the inclusion of people of diverse ethnic backgrounds, religious identities, sexual orientations, and viewpoints.

Some pioneers in the field of diversity argue that broadening the view of diversity has diluted the focus on race to such a degree that discrimination may be overlooked in training. Their beliefs are based on the idea that including other groups within the context of diversity decreases the potential for change, since discrimination against religion, sexual orientation, culture, etc., do not elicit a reaction that is comparable to racial issues.

Recent research indicates that a large proportion of Americans share an anti-gay/anti-lesbian attitude, stemming primarily from religious beliefs. The attitudes and beliefs surrounding those of differing sexual orientations have become more tolerant in recent years, however. This is evidenced by the fact that a movie about two cowboy lovers, Brokeback Mountain, was successful and recent legislation was introduced in an effort to protect the rights of the LGBTQ+ community.

Multiculturalism is an educational philosophy that considers the diverse ways that people identify as cultural beings. One of its primary goals is to consider how each of the identity groups may have unresolved racial biases and cover the distinctions between the many different identity groups in an effective way. A current focus of diversity education is centered on educating White people about White privilege. Most of the training/educational platforms involve challenging White people to consider how social, political, and economic power can be used to promote equality. It is important for DEI consultants and HR professionals to take a critical approach concerning issues of White privilege, multiculturalism and racism. It's also essential to recognize that organizations vary in their diversity education needs. The role of the trainer is to determine which type of educational efforts may be necessary, whether focused on race, religion, sexual orientation or discrimination. Diversity professionals who possess critical self-reflection skills and an ability to facilitate issues that are beyond the breadth of their personal experiences have more potential to accurately assess a situation and prescribe the most appropriate approach.

By now, it should be clear that a discussion of diversity in the US should encompass every possible color of the rainbow. Considering the viewpoints of Catholic or Jew, Gay or Straight, European, African, Hispanic or Asian is not enough. Rather, to fully understand the complex nature of diversity, it's essential to recognize that the US contains a rich cultural tapestry, woven from many different beliefs, backgrounds, preferences and viewpoints. To be effective, modern diversity trainers need to be adept at communicating with people of various racial and cultural backgrounds. The goal, of course, is to facilitate discussions and trainings within a multicultural context, giving each identity group the attention it deserves.

Globalization has created many issues, including making DEI education and training efforts more complex. For example, the term

"African American" is not only racially insensitive but also a misnomer, as Black and White Africans both migrate to the United States. Within just one organization, there may be employees from the former Yugoslavia, refugees from Somalia, guest workers from India, and people with limited English-speaking skills. Along with religious diversity, these are only a few of the challenges associated with modern diversity education.

To remove productivity barriers in the workplace, diversity professionals such as Judith Katz focus on promoting inclusive organizations. This helps ensure that historically excluded groups are not at a disadvantage in the workplace. Another recent change that has been the center of a significant amount of debate concerns a newfound emphasis on diversity education instead of diversity training. One likely explanation for the change is that a mention of diversity training has historically elicited a negative reaction. A significant amount of attention has been paid to the debate, but it essentially boils down to semantics over how to refer to a broad range of activities that allow people to learn about and discuss different characteristics related to social identity. Referring to these activities as diversity education is preferable, as it mitigates negative responses and more accurately represents what DEI programs are all about.

More importantly, this change allows for a distinction between training and education. It's significant insofar as it allows for a distinction between the various practices used by organizations. It is also worthwhile to note how these practices have evolved over time. Previous generations would have been puzzled about the idea of a "chief diversity officer." The fact that positions such as these now exist is a solid indicator that positive changes have taken place. Such changes help to reconstruct a history of racial equity initiatives in organizations.

Diversity Pioneers

As the approach to diversity continues to evolve, many companies are embracing the idea of having diversity professionals on staff. Diversity professionals are responsible for leading diversity initiatives within their organizations, thereby providing employees with an opportunity to share their opinions, experiences, and perspectives. They often hold titles such as chief diversity officer or vice president of diversity, with responsibilities including leading company-wide diversity initiatives. Some diversity professionals also serve as educators, tasked with leading sensitivity-awareness trainings and other programs. Others work closely with human resource professionals and function more like consultants. Regardless of the role and/or responsibilities, these positions are becoming increasingly prevalent as businesses recognize that diversity is an asset that can increase productivity. Many business leaders are realizing that diversity equates to more capital, so they are hiring diversity professionals who can help the organizations continually improve their employment practices. Diversity pioneers laid the foundation for modern diversity leaders. Diversity leaders include those who have been in the profession for over 20 years, whether acting as consultants or working in-house.

The list below is based on data collected by Diversity Training University International students. The list below includes a few diversity pioneers from the United States:

- Elsie Cross
- Price Cobb
- Sybil Evans
- John Fernandez
- Lee Gardenswartz
- Louis Griggs
- Ed Hubbard
- Judith Katz
- Francis Kendall
- Fred Miller
- Patricia Pope
- Ann Rowe
- Donna Springer
- Roosevelt Thomas

A relatively small number of diversity pioneers received formal training prior to entering the business world. Lewis Griggs, a graduate of Stanford University who holds an MBA, is one such pioneer. Judith Katz, with a doctorate from the University of Massachusetts that focused on race relations as well as many years of teaching in the University of Oklahoma Human Relations Program, is another. The author (who?), a cultural-cognitive psychologist, teaches culture and diversity at the University of California, San Diego. In 1986 he received his doctorate. For nearly two decades, he taught cultural competence to aspiring diversity professionals. Each pioneer in diversity has been forced to learn how to navigate the landmines of diversity issues while on the front line working as consultants and trainers. The pioneers may have lacked credentials that are specific to diversity work; however, their effort, tenacity and experience have been a substantial factor in leveling the playing field.

Raising the Bar

After becoming a student activist for social justice in the late 1960s, Judith Katz began working on diversity issues. She started her career by focusing on racism from the perspective of White Americans. At this time, a variety of organizations were attempting to diversify their workforce to comply with affirmative action laws and avoid lawsuits. Many companies contracted with independent diversity consultants to create diversity training programs that would help them recruit and retain minority workers, especially women and Black employees.

Judith Katz

According to Katz, diversity training often focused on Black-White relations, gender issues and sexism. Very little attention was paid to other groups, such as Latinx, Asians, and people with disabilities. Katz also realized that the business case for implementing diversity initiatives was more focused on the moral aspect of doing so, instead of the bottom line. This is part of the explanation for why it was difficult at the time to achieve real organizational change.

Businesses now view diversity as a key business driver rather than something that is essential from an ethical standpoint. This has been a positive change in many ways, as it has shifted the focus of diversity education from a confrontational approach to a key business strategy that has the potential to generate acceptance and opportunity for all. Researchers have reported the traditional approach to diversity education encourages compliance and increases awareness of diversity issues. Leaders who have applied a confrontational approach have found that, in many cases, these efforts fall on deaf ears, increasing resistance from stakeholders and reducing their ability to make changes to their organization's culture. More and more, however, organizational leaders are moving beyond compliance to effect real change in their work environments.

A discussion of the DEI movement would be incomplete without mentioning the concerns that diversity leaders have held and the obstacles they have faced. Diversity initiatives, of course, can be sabotaged if the leaders responsible for implementing these initiatives only pay lip service to the idea of diversity instead of making real attempts to achieve significant changes in their organizations.

In the case where real efforts are not being made, it's common for diversity leaders to end up having to shoulder the full weight of the diversity initiative. It is easy to see why this could lead to burnout, ultimately hindering any progress that could have been made in furthering the initiative. A leader, after all, is just a person without the support of the team. If a diversity leader does not have the support and resources they need to accomplish diversity initiatives and goals, their efforts will be ineffective. A lack of resources and support point to a larger issue: namely, a lack of interest. In a scenario such as this, it is highly unlikely that any DEI initiative will be successful.

Some argue the management of diversity programs is a highly political role. As one would expect, this could make a DEI position extremely difficult, demanding and lonely. Diversity officers are expected to "raise the bar," similar to how their fellow organizational leaders are expected to perform. An effective way for organizations to achieve DEI goals would be to encourage employees to promote inclusion, especially managers and supervisors. Katz believes leaders of diversity initiatives need to raise the bar for expectations in delivering results. That way, organizations will be more likely to support their diversity officers. It is seldom considered that linking bonuses and merit pay to clear DEI metrics would raise the bar of expectations.

Valuing diversity has been a central concept in the movement for social justice. Language scholar Lewis Griggs introduced the idea of valuing people for their diversity in the early 1980s, but those close to him thought it was "too touchy-feely." Even his African American colleagues advised against using such language, warning that White Americans were not ready to embrace people for their differences. Fortunately, Griggs had a vision.

Griggs is a White American of European descent who came to diversity work after facing up to his limitations. Griggs says, "I had been doing international training during the early 1980s, and I realized that people from other countries had more knowledge about me as an American than I had about them. This meant they had more power over me in our interactions. I discovered how ethnocentric I was. Then I asked myself, 'If I'm ethnocentric about people from other countries, then am I also ethnocentric here in the States?'"

Griggs developed a series of videos on the subject of valuing diversity, which greatly influenced the field. He then developed one of the first online diversity training programs. Lewis created the annual diversity conference that is now run by the Society of Human Resource Management. Thanks to Lewis, more organizations are embracing the idea that we need to value our differences.

Avoiding a Backlash

In the 1980s, a number of prominent universities and colleges began forcing students to take diversity courses as part of the general education curriculum. Stanford University and California State

University at Fullerton, for example, made cultural diversity courses a mandatory component of their general education requirements. Academics debated whether or not the canon needed protection from such an inclusion.

The author (Griggs?) found himself in the middle of the culture war while teaching at a large public university, where most students were politically conservative. He had a joint appointment in Ethnic Studies and Psychology, and his training made it easy to integrate cultural differences into his Developmental, Social, and Cognitive Psychology courses. He also taught mandatory general education diversity courses. The primarily European American, politically conservative students had a difficult time accepting the required courses. The students resisted less as the courses integrated into the curricula over the years, but many continued to struggle with the material due to the difficulty of accepting values and beliefs that were different from their own.

Once universities realized they could no longer avoid the issue of racial inclusion, efforts were made to remedy past mistakes. To recruit people of color in larger numbers, many universities adopted policies that would attract more diverse groups of students. Recruitment policies were viewed as the first step toward creating a more inclusive environment. After the number of recruits from diverse cultural backgrounds increased, however, it became clear that retention and graduation were major problems. As a result, many institutions of higher learning were forced to revise their recruitment practices.

The author (?) witnessed unprecedented gains in attracting students of historically excluded groups. Unfortunately, changes in leadership and the economic climate threatened every step forward. The lesson is that sustainable DEI initiatives require ongoing commitment from leadership. Their role is to remove the barriers that could result in a reversion to the old ways of doing business. DEI initiatives should be a part of the broader organizational strategy. This would help to avoid the retracement of previously held beliefs and practices and continue driving the organization into a brighter future.

The efforts of the pioneers should not be forgotten, as their ability to navigate economic, political, and global changes required vision, tenacity, inventiveness and creativity. Their capacity to identify solutions for old problems, often with a lack of resources and funding, provide a number of invaluable lessons. The pioneers exerted a positive impact through their bravery and courage, creating a paradigm for DEI leaders to follow moving forward.

4

Racial Diversity

*I never had an occasion to question color; therefore, I
only saw myself as what I was ... a human being.*
—Sidney Poitier

The following is a firsthand account of an organization with racial diversity and discrimination issues. It was provided by Loni Mendez, a professional writer, HR consultant, and developmental editor. Her experience is below:

"I worked for a large pharmaceutical company in the HR department. I had started out with this company as a contractor, and after one year I was brought on as an employee in a high-level independent contributor role. I remained with the company for two more years after becoming an employee. During my three years of service with this organization, my performance reviews were always good at the very least. There was never any negative feedback, and the progression of my salary was indicative of this. When I transitioned from a contractor to company employee, I was brought in at $10,000 more than the amount I was earning in the interim position. My annual increases for the time that I remained with the company reflected my performance as well.

After being with the company for about three years, I was contacted by a headhunter. I was not looking to change jobs at the time, but this was and still is a common practice. Headhunters find potential candidates through associations, social media, and referrals, and they contact you with these attractive offers to try and win you over so that you'd leave your current employer and accept a position with one of their client companies. I was invited to interview with another pharmaceutical company, but I declined. The recruiter didn't stop there. He went on to list out the details of what the other company was offering and pleaded with me to at least accept the interview. I eventually folded and agreed to at least meet with the hiring manager. After the meeting, I thought about how accepting the position would allow me the opportunity to do some design work. My area of expertise was compensation, and in the role I was in at that time, I was responsible for day-to-day administration of programs and had very little involvement in compensation program design and development.

A week later, I was contacted and offered the position. I was torn. There was a part of me that wanted to accept the position, but I was happy where I was. I had learned so much over the three years, and this company was one that was at the cutting edge of emerging methodology and technology. It was a company that was leading the way and setting trends in the industry across all its functions. I approached the woman whom I reported to; she was a director. I let her know I had an offer on the table, but I loved working there. I wanted a little insight regarding my future with the company. Her response was that I should speak with our global head, who was based in Europe.

Before I continue, I want to shed some light on just how the European headquarters of this company operated. Aside from the fact that African American and Latinx managers were almost nonexistent, particularly in Europe but also here in the US, I had witnessed innuendos that referenced race or color on more than one occasion during my time there. Additionally, the European offices were so different than the US when it came to fairness and equity that they used salary survey data that was compiled based on age, sex, and other criteria that would be deemed as discriminatory in the US.

The day after speaking with my director, I reached out to my global head to have a conversation about my future with the company. Keep in mind that I was not asking for promises from them; I just wanted to entertain a

conversation about my options over the years ahead. He replied, "You will never make manager at this company." This response was a surprise, because in my twenty years of experience in the workforce, especially since for half of those years I worked in HR, I had heard of people being provided with the areas that they needed to develop that would prepare them for promotion. But this manager did not have any recommendations for steps I could take that would prepare me. He was simply saying that it would never—and he did use the word never—happen. With my performance being above average for my entire time there, I was left wondering if this was just business as usual, which would explain the glass ceiling in the organization for minorities, or if it was something personal. Clearly, that comment was not based on my performance, as no performance issues were ever documented. If I was not demonstrating consistent, sound performance, then why did I receive the increases to my salary every year?

That next day I accepted the position and submitted my two-week notice to the company. At the time, there was some talk about a diversity and inclusion role that was being created, but it was at the beginning stages. That was sixteen years ago, and I sincerely hope that by now this pharmaceutical giant has recognized the need to address the cultural differences between the two countries and the lack of opportunities for minority employees."

Loni Mendez
Professional Writer l Developmental Editor l HR Consultant Global HR Concepts LLC

Modern workplaces are moving toward a culture that values diversity and welcomes everyone. A partial explanation for the shift is that creating a more accepting environment has the potential to improve organizational effectiveness and boost employee morale. Although DEI initiatives are gaining acceptance, many organizations continue to receive negative reports about racial and ethnic discrimination, gender bias, unfair hiring practices, and a lack of inclusion.

One of the best ways to fight prejudice and bigotry is to educate people about racial/cultural diversity, gender identity, sexual orientation, neurodiversity, disability, and more. Attractive diverse representatives to the staff helps people learn more about each other. Doing so has the potential to bring people together. When the staff already has a diverse talent base, other people are more likely to want to join the organization. This can help to breathe new life into a business and/or workplace.

The Equal Employment Opportunity Commission says that employers pay an average of $112.7 million each year to settle charges of racial discrimination. Over the last 10 years, the number of cases of racial discrimination has increased. At first glance, the numbers do not seem concerning. After realizing that many instances of racial discrimination are not reported, however, the case becomes clear that that the real numbers are probably much higher.

Companies should make a business case for diversity that lists the benefits, such as:

- Gains in worker happiness and productivity
- Reduced turnover costs
- Fewer fights and complaints
- Access to new markets/income sources
- Higher levels or capital and employee productivity
- Increased creativity
- Stronger innovation and inventiveness
- Reputational benefits
- More capacity to change and adapt in a globalized world
- Decreased risk exposure from noncompliance

It is important to note that, when DEI measures are in place, employees are more likely to buy into the organizational mission. A spike in engagement from employees can lead to higher levels of productivity and retention; it can also add to the effectiveness of recruitment efforts.

Important Terminology

To develop DEI policies and practices for use in the workplace, it's important to gain an understanding about the proper use and definition of common words and phrases. This is the first step toward creating a positive, productive environment where people will feel comfortable having a conversation about race relations and racial diversity in the workplace.

- Racial discrimination – In the workplace, this occurs when an employee is treated unfairly because of their race or ethnic background. Instances of racial discrimination could include passing over someone that deserved a promotion, a raise or a new position within the company; basically any action that could be viewed as biased against an individual due to their race.
- Ethnic group – This term references groups of people with similar cultural, linguistic and geographical roots.
- Ethnic minority – Contrary to what many believe, this term not only refers to a small group of people, it also refers to any ethnic group with a historically low level of power in society, politics and/or the economy.
- Implicit bias – This concept is based on how unconscious beliefs and perceptions about other groups have an impact on the way people respond to others.
- Inclusion – As the name implies, this refers to activities designed to include people and groups of all levels in the organization in shaping policies and decision-making.

Of course, there are many other common phrases and terms that should be understood within the context of DEI initiatives, however, space constraints prohibit a comprehensive list.

Who is Responsible for Diversity Implementation?

Once an agreement has been reached about the importance of DEI practices in the workplace, the work has only just begun. The next step is to identify the person or persons who will be responsible for implementing these policies, as well as how DEI practices can be effectively promoted on a broader, organizational level.

To stop discrimination in the workplace, employers should act as facilitators and sources of information. Employees on every level of the organization should receive education and training on diversity issues. Enforcement is another item of concern. Regulations are already in place to ensure the fair treatment of workers, but regulations are nothing without the enforcement actions to back them up. It's also important to note that, if an employee raises an issue about the treatment they are receiving and that instance is documented, the organization can be subject to a variety of negative outcomes from the EEOC if no action is taken. Learning more about diversity can make the entire organization function at a higher level, benefiting everyone from the owners to the staff and other key stakeholders.

Employees and groups that are focused on safeguarding the rights of employees should continue to advocate for the adoption of policies that encourage racial and ethnic diversity. It is also essential to ensure that all workers have the same opportunities at every stage of the employment cycle, from recruitment and hiring to promotions and retirement. Employees have an important role in raising awareness about racial bias. And, if someone raises a valid concern or complaint, coworkers should support each other. In the instance of a complaint, any form of retaliation against that individual should be avoided, as the EEOC takes these actions very seriously and there are a variety of protections in place for whistleblowers.

In short, the goal of making a positive change will require an ongoing effort from everyone in the organization.

5

Cultural Diversity

*Embracing cultural diversity is like a new great way to
experience our beautiful world new again, again, and
again from new perspectives. Your life will become richer
and richer every time you see it from a different lens.*
— Brian Ka Chan

The world is a mosaic of people from all different walks of life and backgrounds. In every corner of the globe, there are people with different racial backgrounds, different identities, religions, cultures and languages. This diversity is what makes the world so beautiful and unique.

Each person has a unique story to tell. Interacting with people from a variety of backgrounds allows us to learn more about our own personalities, as well as the world around us. By celebrating our differences, we can learn to appreciate the beauty in everyone and build a more tolerant, understanding world.

Culture shapes who we are as individuals. Our identity, behaviors and values add up to our overall "way of being," which is informed by the culture in which we were raised. Understanding that there are many different cultures in the world, it's important to be respectful when we encounter people from other backgrounds. There are a variety of different ways to show respect. A critical step in the mission to achieve effective, respectful communications would be to learn more about an individual's culture prior to the first interaction.

There are a number of important steps people must take to become more accepting of cultural diversity and understand its benefits. It starts with considering the fact the world contains a richly woven tapestry of differing cultures and ethnicities. Each culture has its own unique set of values, beliefs and traditions that are worth respecting. Another important aspect of cultural diversity is the acknowledgment that all cultural expressions are valid. This means every culture has something to contribute to the global community. It's also essential to understand the value that different cultures have to offer. Increased levels of understanding can result from empowering diverse groups to contribute their unique perspectives to the global community. Finally, celebrating the differences between cultures is one of the most effective ways to encourage people to be more accepting of cultural diversity. This means we should not only tolerate different cultures, we should also celebrate them for their differences.

There are many different examples of cultural diversity. Some of the more notable examples of diversity include different languages, religions and cultures. There are over 7,000 different languages spoken around the world, each with its own unique set of idioms and expressions. Additionally, there are over 4,000 different religions practiced worldwide, each with its own set of customs and traditions. Finally, there are countless different cultures across the globe, each with its own unique food, music, art, and way of life. It's also important to note that the traditions of many different cultures overlap in a variety of ways, and this only adds to the diversity.

All of these cultures and traditions blend together into what we call cultural diversity. To support cultural diversification in the public and private sector, it is essential to have multi-lingual teams, diverse age ranges working together, anti-discrimination policies, and other practices that encourage diversity.

Cultural Diversity in Education

Cultural diversity is important in many aspects of life, but it can be even more important in an educational setting. Students all over the world should have the right to experience the same quality of education. A number of key benefits can occur when institutions believe in the power of diversity. It is widely accepted that diversity makes the classroom a better place to learn for both students and teachers. Many of our differences become immediately apparent after walking into a study room or lecture hall, for example. Mentioning these differences, of course, is not the same as telling people to accept their differences. The point is that it is a good idea to have a frank discussion about individual values and beliefs in an academic setting, as doing so can lead to increased levels of understanding. There are many research-backed benefits to having a diverse educational team, such as better conflict resolution and problem-solving skills. Having a diverse educational team also allows for a better understanding of the material being taught; better use and allocation of resources; higher student perceptions of personal competence and professional commitment; more constructive feedback on work initiatives; higher self-esteem and better attitudes toward learning.

Academic institutions have always played a significant role in fostering tolerance and making room for different cultures. Cultural diversity training and education is important for all schools, colleges and universities. It should be at the center of every curriculum.

The following list includes a variety of concepts, ideas and educational methods that were designed to support cultural diversity initiatives.

Deep Learning

Deep learning pertains to evaluating the complexity of the world. By looking deeper and asking questions, more insights can be gained on how our beliefs fit into our lives as a whole and how they affect the people around us. Deep learners use evidence, reasoning, creativity and communication skills to identify solutions for difficult problems. They are very independent and have a strong sense of who they are as students. This educational method allows for essential learning opportunities, both from a standpoint of what works and what does not. Deep learners work carefully with others and apply a tremendous amount of thought to every action. Deep learners recognize that their beliefs should be able to change in response to new insights and information. They also acknowledge that other people have different beliefs and viewpoints.

Confidence and Growth

Research shows that students and employees are more likely to feel confident about their skills and the way they express themselves if they have the opportunity to learn in an environment with many different cultures. It's also more likely that people will consider taking on a leadership role in this type of environment.

Preparation for the Future

Cultural diversity in the classroom can lead to a deeper awareness of various cultures, and this can provide students with an array of positive outcomes. Better communication skills, of course, are an essential factor for success in today's multi-ethnic society. Students need to be able to work with people from all walks of life, especially as the world becomes more and more globalized.

More Empathy

When students have an opportunity to learn about different cultures in the classroom and workplace, they have more potential to understand and collaborate with people from different backgrounds. This helps to eliminate biases and discrimination, which is important for the future.

Supporting Cultural Diversity

The best way to support cultural diversity is to be intentional. Reflecting on personal beliefs and assumptions could be a great place to start. Doing so can help to gain an understanding of how to recognize and respect cultural differences. A few moments of reflection can also illuminate whether implicit biases are having an influence on decision-making.

It is important to recognize that we are all exposed to cultural messages every day—through the media, schools, workplaces, and our homes. Being surrounded by the same people in similar environments can reduce the potential for learning more about different beliefs. In this type of scenario, it can be easy to forget that other perspectives exist.

The easiest way to challenge personally held cultural biases is by acknowledging they exist. Learning more about how these biases influence personal relationships is essential. All of these elements are critical signposts on the pathway toward understanding, as they can help gain awareness of how beliefs, actions, statements and opinions can cause another person to experience discomfort or pain.

Researching an unfamiliar culture to find similarities and differences is another important step. Doing so can support a deeper understanding of the importance of encouraging a diverse community that represents all perspectives, races, religions, and backgrounds. If no effort is paid to gain understanding, the risk of spreading harmful negative stereotypes is increased significantly. Human beings have inhabited the Earth for thousands of years. Over the years, we have formed communities, shared cultures and learned to live with each other, which could make any of us think that we are familiar with cultural diversity. Similar to how a drop of water in a vast ocean can only be truly understood in relation to its surroundings, so too can the concept of cultural diversity only be truly understood in relation to the interplay of global factors and themes. Now is the time for an open, honest discussion about the different aspects of cultural diversity.

Cultural Competence

Culture is a learned set of behaviors and beliefs, passed on from one generation to the next. Typically, culture is transmitted in the form of stories and myths, which people often accept without question. The culture that is present in a certain region or place can be interpreted as the character and personality of the people who live there. The term culture has been derived from the Latin word cultures. This means cultivation, which basically refers to the act of growing something or developing it. Culture essentially refers to the identity of a certain group of people. It has a pervasive impact on the way individuals choose to relate with others and the society as a whole. The definition of culture is multifaceted. One aspect of culture is cultural competence, which is the ability of an individual to act in accordance with their cultural heritage, as well as modify their behavior to adapt to new situations, norms and beliefs.

Cultural competence provides an advantage in society because it provides the individual with an opportunity to gain a deeper understanding of closely held beliefs and ideas, as well as the beliefs and ideas embraced by the broader society. Cultural competence allows for an appreciation of different customs, traditions, beliefs, ideas, values, and norms, which vary from one culture to another. Having a more substantial knowledge base related to how people from different cultural backgrounds work and communicate can supplement a leader's ability to adapt and respond to different situations, making that individual a more effective leader.

Cultural competence encompasses four aspects:

- Awareness – Before it is possible to understand the cultural orientations of other people, individuals should have an understanding of the culture in which they were raised.
- Attitude – Being able to adapt to different cultures requires an open-minded attitude toward cultural differences. A person demonstrating cultural competence is able to acknowledge the value of differing cultural beliefs and practices. Having a nonjudgmental attitude that is accepting and flexible is also essential.
- Knowledge – Cultural competence requires a thorough knowledge of the culture in which an individual was raised, as well as an understanding of disparate cultural traditions. This knowledge should encompass the beliefs of other cultures related to gender roles, class systems, religious traditions, family structures, communication styles, and language use.

- Skills – By working to attain the first three aspects of cultural competence, an individual can build a skill set that allows him or her to effectively interact with individuals from diverse cultures.

Cultural Competence Continuum

The cultural competence continuum is a set of principles and practices that are designed to increase the understanding, effectiveness, and sensitivity of practitioners in working with individuals or groups with differing cultural backgrounds. It applies to all persons, organizations, and institutions that serve diverse populations. The model is designed to help professionals understand the concepts of cultural competence, achieve different levels of competency, and leverage strategies for achieving greater competency in providing culturally competent services.

Cultural Destructiveness

Cultural destructiveness occurs when a person or group of people come to believe they are more important than a larger community or society as a whole. These beliefs often result in actions that are harmful to the individual, the group, and the broader society.

The main characteristic of cultural destructiveness involves a separation between "us" and "them." The idea that a person or group is somehow better than other groups is culturally destructive. This can result in the belief that the lives of one group have more value than the lives of the people in other groups.

For example, a political party may decide there should be one set of rules for their group and different rules for other groups. This could result in legislation passing that helps their group at the expense of everyone else.

Cultural Incapacity

Cultural incapacity refers to a lack of understanding, awareness, or appreciation of the beliefs and practices inherent with other cultures. This can spiral to an extreme where those who are unaware and uninformed about other cultures form misguided assumptions based on their personally held beliefs and norms. Cultural incapacity often results in stereotypes, prejudice, and bigotry.

A common example occurs when a person from one culture visits another and does something that is considered rude. Without a position of knowledge about the other culture to draw from, the likelihood of unintentionally violating a cultural norm increases significantly.

Cultural Blindness

Cultural blindness describes the inability of a company or individual to understand the culture of a certain market. Success becomes impossible in different geographical regions when a company or individual is unable to see beyond their personal cultural perspective and ways of doing business. Cultural blindness can result in significant opportunity costs and severely impede a company's ability to make headway in different regions and/or countries.

Treating people differently as a response to a perceived lack of ability is cultural blindness. The concept is not limited to race or ethnicity, however. Cultural blindness can pertain to gender, age, education level, sexual orientation and religious beliefs—even socioeconomic status.

Cultural Proficiency

Cultural proficiency is the ability to engage, communicate and work effectively across cultures. This is a strategic ability that is essential for helping an organization reach its full potential, both internally and externally.

For example, employees who are accustomed to communicating in loud, assertive ways may be viewed as harsh or insensitive by people from other cultures who prefer more subtle forms of communication.

A lack of cultural proficiency can lead to miscommunications and misunderstandings. This can result in a variety of negative outcomes, all of which have the potential to damage organizational effectiveness.

There are several resources pertaining to cultural competency, one of which is the Purnell Model. A framework for understanding cultural communication and organizational dynamics, the Purnell Model emphasizes the practice of using "cultural ripples" to achieve effective intercultural interactions and relationships.

The Purnell Model provides a framework for cultural competence through a process that starts by connecting with the culture, participating in the culture, analyzing cultural data, and developing questions. The next phases involve verifying results, applying knowledge to practice, and evaluating outcomes.

Cultural Identity

Cultural identity refers to the unique characteristics that make up a person or group of people. This term essentially refers to the perceptions a group maintains about their culture, as well as how others perceive it. These characteristics include language, religion, customs, traditions and practices, heroes, symbols, and values.

Cultural identity can be defined as a positive or negative awareness of the individual or the group as a whole. People with the same cultural identity belong to a group whose members share the same beliefs and values. In this way, cultural identity involves both an individual's acceptance of other people and their acceptance by the group.

In some cases, cultural identity can be confused with nationality or ethnicity. The difference is that national identity tends to focus on political allegiance and ethnicity instead of biological descent.

The notion of culture is constantly evolving. Cultural identities are shaped by the values, norms and beliefs that hold society together, such as laws and institutions, history, art, stories, experiences, social behaviors, religions, languages, traditions and rituals. Culture is a complex fabric with many different factors. Some of the other aspects associated with cultural identity include technology, weapons, clothing styles, food preferences and preparation methods, music, and architecture.

Identities are created by conscious decisions, such as voting for a certain political party. Many unconscious decisions also relate to forming a cultural identity, including the language that is spoken or the geographic location.

Cultural Assimilation

Cultural assimilation is the process by which a minority group or culture starts to resemble the norms and rules associated with a dominant culture. Cultural assimilation may involve either a quick or gradual change in cultural values, customs, and behaviors. It can either be voluntary or a forced change exerted on a minority group.

Originally, the term assimilation was used to replace the term acculturation. The term acculturation implies that two cultures are coming together, while the term assimilation suggests one culture is becoming dominant over another. As such, the term assimilation is now more commonly used in academic fields such as anthropology rather than in sociology.

In some cases, cultural assimilation can involve either voluntary integration or forced integration, such as with Indigenous People and African Americans. The example of forced integration is illustrated by when Native American children were forced to attend government-sponsored boarding schools designed to erase their heritage and adopt them into European American society.

The end result of cultural assimilation does not have to be homogenization. Though some groups and cultures assimilate through practices such as intermarriage or adoption of new cultural practices, many desire to preserve aspects of their culture's identity.

Assimilation can assume a variety of forms, including:

- Ethnic assimilation – This refers to the adoption of a different culture by an ethnic group—for example, when immigrants adapt to the customs and language of a new country.
- Cultural assimilation – This occurs when a culture adopts the customs and norms of another culture. An example of cultural assimilation is when groups of immigrants are expected to adopt the customs and language of a new country.

- Mosaic integration – This form of cultural assimilation allows newcomers to keep certain aspects of their culture while living in a new country or region.
- Rapid assimilation – This type of cultural assimilation occurs when one group of people is forced to yield to the culture of another group more quickly than they might like. Examples include military conquest, slavery, forced immigration, and genocide.

It is important to point out that some individuals may resist assimilating to a new culture. An individual such as this may be deemed a "cultural separatist" or "cultural conservative." These individuals are likely to resist learning a new language and hold on to old ways as much as possible.

Tolerance of other cultures doesn't necessarily lead to assimilation, as some groups maintain distinct identities while living in a different culture or region. But when one culture becomes dominant, the unique traits of that culture are more likely to be absorbed by other cultures within the same society.

The opposite of assimilation is cultural isolation—a phenomenon in which an individual or group maintains its own identity in spite of being surrounded by other people and cultures. A classic example of cultural isolation is provided by the Amish, who have maintained their cultural identity for centuries despite being surrounded by American culture.

Assimilation and cultural isolation are two sides of the same coin. When someone is isolated from mainstream society, that individual has no choice but to remain true to previously held beliefs and values—the assimilation process becomes impossible. On the other hand, when a group is forced to assimilate—as slaves were in the United States—new cultural influences may increase the tendency to lean toward isolation.

Cultural Diffusion

Cultural diffusion is the spread of cultural ideas, practices, and products. The term also relates to the transfer of ideas, information and technology within a culture or between different cultures. Diffusion is a natural process common to all human societies that encompasses the spread of religions, inventions, culture, politics, and technological innovations. It can be defined as "the spread of new ideas and practices through certain channels over time."

Diffusion has occurred throughout history by means of a variety of processes. These include expansion through conquest of foreign territories; movement of peoples; immigration; trade; travel; communication, such as the internet; and colonization.

There are many examples of cultural diffusion, including:

- Material – This pertains to the exchange of physical items, such as the spread of coffee and coffeehouses throughout Europe and eventually the world.
- Religious – This refers to the dissemination of belief systems, ideologies and rituals. An example would be how Christianity, Buddhism, and Islam spread across much of the world.
- Behavioral – Activities that people participate in together in groups, such as soccer, baseball, and basketball, provide an example of behavioral cultural diffusion.
- Institutional - The way that fast-food restaurants like McDonald's and KFC have gained popularity around the world is an example of institutional cultural diffusion, as it involves social structures, business practices and laws.

Cultural Isolation

Cultural isolation is a term that has gained prominence in the last few years. It has gained relevance in modern society because, even though technology has allowed us to connect with each other in ways we could have only dreamed of in prior years, it is also creating divisions that did not previously exist. Thus, technology that was intended to bring us closer together is also driving us apart.

Cultural isolation happens when a person or group is cut off from the broader society in which they live. It typically refers to cultural groups who have been isolated and marginalized by governments, cultures, or societies. There are several causes of cultural isolation. One is the geographic separation of a cultural group from the surrounding population. This can happen as a result of language barriers, physical barriers or restrictions placed on a cultural group by the surrounding culture. Another cause of cultural isolation is the lack of political autonomy of a group. When a government seeks to exert control over certain groups within its territory, it may do so by isolating those groups from others through segregation laws, physical relocation, and movement restrictions.

Treating those who are culturally isolated with respect and compassion can help to prevent them from feeling devalued. This can improve social cohesion and increase acceptance of diverse cultures within society.

Cultural Imperialism

Cultural imperialism is used to describe the spread of a culture to another country. This can happen in many ways. For example, popular music, movies, television shows, and commercials can be exported around the world. These art forms are viewed and imitated by people from other countries who are inspired to create their own versions.

Within the context of cultural imperialism, the spread of one culture to another may be deliberate or unintentional. Whether a slow process that occurs over time or something faster, cultural imperialism can refer to cultural domination or cultural assimilation.

In most cases, cultural imperialism is related to economic factors. Cultural imperialism is often viewed as an act of forced assimilation, such as when a foreign culture is forced upon a native population. In this scenario, the native population may view the action as an effort to conquer them, culturally and economically, through globalization.

Critics argue that exporting Western values and preferences maintains cultural imperialism, using commercialism instead of military force as a means of domination.

Caroline King, PhD

Cultural Relativism

Cultural relativism is the idea that every culture is different and should therefore be judged independently from other cultures. An essential component of this concept is that personally held beliefs, values, and practices are not necessarily better than those held by others. Cultural relativism can be applied to many aspects of life. In fact, cultural relativism has been a part of anthropological study since its inception and it continues to inform the practice. It is also a basic tenet in most world philosophies, religions, and cultures.

The doctrine of cultural relativism is based on the idea that an individual's cultural background will have a significant impact on the values and beliefs that person embraces throughout their life.

Cultural Appropriation

Some argue that it is unethical to try to Westernize other cultures and that members of minority groups should be provided with an opportunity to preserve their cultural identity. However, some argue that working to provide minority groups with a chance to preserve their identity is patronizing, in that it creates harmful outcomes.

Cultural appropriation, as it is understood today, involves the taking of cultural elements from a minority culture by a more dominant culture. This could include the use of traditional clothing, music, dance, art, or cuisine. While cultural appropriation has been a part of human history for centuries, it is often now viewed as a negative phenomenon, as the minority cultures from which the elements are taken often lack power and representation.

Critics of cultural appropriation argue it is a form of exploitation, as the dominant culture often takes from minority cultures without giving anything back. They also argue it can be damaging to the minority cultures from which the elements are taken, as it can lead to their degradation and loss of identity. Others argue that cultural appropriation may simply be a side effect of globalization and/or a result of more people/cultures coming together in a vast melting pot. For those that support this idea, there are many positive examples to be found, solely within the context of American culinary offerings, such as pizza, tacos, sushi and lo Mein.

Japanese Internment Camps in the USA

Any discussion of cultural assimilation, imperialism or appropriation is remiss without mentioning the Japanese Internment Camps, which are a stain on the history of the US. During World War II, President Franklin D. Roosevelt used Executive Order 9066 to relocate individuals of Japanese descent to internment camps. From 1942 to 1945, the US government made it a policy that people of Japanese descent, including US citizens, would be sent to camps where they would be segregated from other people. The incarceration of Japanese Americans is viewed by many as one of the worst violations of American civil rights in the 20th century. The move was partially a response to the attacks on Pearl Harbor and the war that followed.

Executive Order 9066

On February 19, 1942, around three months after Japanese forces bombed Pearl Harbor, President Roosevelt signed Executive Order 9066, which was supposed to stop spies from working in the United States.

In California, Washington and Oregon, where there were large communities of Japanese Americans, the order resulted in the installation of military zones. The next phase of Roosevelt's executive order involved forcing Japanese Americans out of their homes. Around 120,000 people were affected by Executive Order 9066, and most of them were American citizens. Canada soon followed suit, moving 21,000 people of Japanese descent from its west coast. Mexico passed a similar law and in the end, more than 2,250 people of Japanese descent were sent from Peru, Brazil, Chile and Argentina to the United States, against their will. In the US, people of Japanese descent were moved off Terminal Island near the Port of Los Angeles weeks before the order.

Just hours after Pearl Harbor was bombed on December 7, 1941, the FBI rounded up 1,291 religious and community leaders who were Japanese Americans. These individuals were arrested without evidence and their assets were frozen. In January, the people who had been arrested were sent to prison camps in Montana, New Mexico, and North Dakota. Many of them couldn't tell their families where they were, and most of them stayed there for the rest of the war. At the same time, the FBI searched the homes of thousands of Japanese Americans on the West Coast and took things that had been deemed illegal.

A third of the entire Hawaiian population was Japanese. In a panic, some politicians asked for all of them to be arrested. Japanese fishing boats were taken away. Lt. General John L. DeWitt, who was in charge of the Western Defense Command, thought it was important to take control of the civilian population to prevent the occurrence of an attack similar to Pearl Harbor. To make his case, DeWitt wrote a report filled with claims that were known to be false, such as examples of sabotage that had turned out to be the result of cows breaking power lines.

DeWitt told Secretary of War Henry Stimson and Attorney General Francis Biddle they should create military zones and put Japanese people in jail. Italians and Germans were also included in his original plan, but the idea of rounding up Americans of European descent was not as popular. In February of 1942, most of the people who spoke at Congressional hearings, including California Governor Culbert L. Olson and State Attorney General Earl Warren, said all Japanese people should be forcibly removed. Biddle informed the president that relocating so many people to internment camps was unnecessary and smaller, more targeted security measures would be better, but Roosevelt signed the order anyway.

War Relocation Authority

In response to the executive order, around 15,000 Japanese Americans moved out of restricted areas. The people in the inland states were fearful about Japanese Americans moving there. It is unfortunate but not all that surprising that, when the Japanese Americans relocated, they were met with racism almost everywhere they went. Concerns over the idea that the Japanese Americans would never want to leave motivated 10 state governors to publicly state that they were unwelcome. They said that if the states were forced to take them in, then the Japanese Americans should be imprisoned.

In March of 1942, a civilian group called the War Relocation Authority was established to run the plan. Milton S. Eisenhower from the Department of Agriculture was put in charge of the group. Eisenhower only served as president of the War Relocation Authority until June 1942. His decision to resign was based on the fact that he didn't agree with locking up people he thought were innocent.

Relocation to "Assembly Centers"

On March 24th, 1942, the Army started relocating the Japanese Americans. People were provided with a notice of six days to dispose of any item they would not be able to carry. Everyone who had one sixteenth of Japanese blood or more had to leave. That number included 17,000 children under 10, as well as several thousand elderly and disabled people. Near their homes, Japanese Americans went to places called "Assembly

Centers." From there, they were taken to a "Relocation Center," where they might stay for a few months before being moved to a "Wartime Residence," where they would remain for the duration of the war.

Assembly Centers were usually placed in remote areas. In many cases, buildings and other installations that were never intended for housing people were used after some rudimentary modifications. These buildings and installations included fairgrounds, race tracks, horse stalls and cow sheds. At the Pacific International Livestock Exposition Facilities in Portland, Oregon, for example, around 3,000 people were housed in the livestock pavilion.

The Santa Anita Assembly Center was a de facto city with 18,000 prisoners, 8,500 of whom lived in stables. It was only a few miles northeast of Los Angeles. In most of these places, there was never enough food and the bathrooms were unsanitary.

Life in "Assembly Centers"

Prisoners were allowed to work at Assembly Centers, but it was forbidden for them to earn more than an Army private. People could work as doctors, teachers, laborers, or mechanics. A few of the Assembly Centers had factories that made camouflage nets, which gave people jobs. Over 1,000 Japanese Americans who were in prison were sent to other states to work on farms during the summer. It's also worth noting that over 4,000 Japanese Americans who were in jail were let out so they could attend college.

Conditions in "Relocation Centers"

There were 10 prison camps the government had inappropriately named "Relocation Centers." These camps included homes for more than one family. People from Tule Lake, California were called dissidents and sent to a special prison camp there. Several Relocation Centers had jobs to offer from net factories. One Relocation Center was the site of a factory where models of naval ships were made. There were also factories in some of the Relocation Centers that made clothes, mattresses and cabinets for use in other prison camps.

Violence in Prison Camps

Unrest and violence were common in the prison camps. In Lordsburg, New Mexico, prisoners were brought to the camp at night by train. They were forced to walk the remaining two miles to get to the camp. On the evening of July 27, 1942, while Toshio Kobata and Hirota Isomura were out walking, a sentry shot and killed them because he thought they were trying to escape. Later, Japanese Americans said the two old men were hurt and had been struggling on the way to Lordsburg. The Army's court martial board decided the sentry was not guilty.

On August 4, 1942, there was a riot at the Santa Anita Assembly Center because there was not enough food to go around. Six men assaulted Fred Tayama, leader of the Japanese American Citizens League (JACL), at the Manzanar War Relocation Center in California. Tensions had been mounting due to the fact that many Japanese Americans believed that JACL members were providing support for the American government. A large crowd had gathered to ask for the release of Harry Ueno, who was taken into custody for allegedly assaulting Tayama. Fearful of a riot, police used tear gas on the crowd. James Ito died as a result of the chaos and several other people were hurt. Jim Kanegawa, who was only 21 at the time, was injured during the protest and passed away five days later as a result. At the Topaz Relocation Center, military police shot and killed 63-year-old prisoner James Hatsuki Wakasa for walking near the perimeter fence. Two months later, a guard opened fire at a couple walking nearby the fence.

In October 1943, the Army sent tanks and soldiers to the northern California Tule Lake Segregation Center to stop protests. Japanese Americans in Tule Lake went on strike to raise awareness about the fact they did not have enough food to eat and the hazardous conditions, which had recently led to an accidental death. On May 24, 1943, a guard shot and killed James Okamoto, a 30-year-old prisoner who drove a construction truck at the same camp.

Trail Blazers

Fred Korematsu, a Japanese American who was 23 years old at the time, was arrested in 1942 because he refused to move to a Japanese prison camp. This led Korematsu to challenge Executive Order 9066, all the way to the Supreme Court. In Korematsu versus the United States, Korematsu's lawyers argued the order was an unconstitutional use of the Fifth Amendment.

Although Korematsu lost the case, he went on to work for civil rights and was eventually honored with the Presidential Medal of Freedom in 1998. California's Fred Korematsu Day was the first holiday in the US to be named after an Asian American. It would take another Supreme Court ruling, however, before the practice of imprisoning Japanese Americans would be halted.

Mitsuye Endo

The Supreme Court's ex parte Mitsuye Endo decision in 1945 put an end to the prison camps. In the case, all the justices agreed that the War Relocation Authority "doesn't have the right to make loyal citizens follow its leave procedure."

Mitsuye Endo was a native of Sacramento, California, whose parents were from Japan. After Endo filed a habeas corpus petition, the government offered to let her go. She turned them down, however, because she wanted her case to delve into the broader issue of Japanese incarceration. It took a year before the Supreme Court made its decision. Prior to making the decision public, the court gave President Truman the chance to start closing the camps. The Supreme Court made its decision public one day after President Truman signed an executive order that eliminated the War Relocation Authority, allowing Japanese Americans to return to their homes.

Reparations

In March 1946, the last camp for Japanese Americans was shut down. In 1976, President Gerald Ford officially got rid of Executive Order 9066. In 1988, President Ronald Reagan signed the Civil Liberties Act. This provided survivors with formal letters of apology, as well as a payment of $20,000 in restitutions to make up for their treatment.

6

Neurodiversity

*The most interesting people you'll find are ones that
don't fit into your average cardboard box. They'll
make what they need, they'll make their own boxes.*
— Dr. Temple Grandin

**The following is a firsthand account of life with a neurodivergent
individual, provided by Janaiah C. von Hassel, a mom, wife, and
neurodiversity advocate.**

Living with Neurodiversity: Unbiased Potential

"When I first came across my husband, I used to be intrigued
with his outlook towards life and nature. On one of our very first
dates, we went trekking together, and while we came back down to
the bottom of the mountain, we sat for about an hour at a picnic. As
we talked, studying each other on a deeper degree, he kept his face

tilted upward in the direction of the sky, but together with his eyes closed, throughout.

Later, I would keep in mind that he's sensitive to sunlight, can feel overwhelmed in inclined conversations, and occasionally processes what people say better when he's not looking straight into their eyes.

I didn't understand a single thing concerning neurodivergence or the autism spectrum then, but I had no bias in how I thought a person must preserve a conversation. Possibly it came from my early life experiences of being around many undiagnosed neurodivergent people however his conduct raised no pink flags for me. Mainly, I was curious. I in no way saw it in a terrible light, and in reality, I discovered him to be one of the most real, articulate, soft-hearted, understanding, compassionate, and empathetic human beings I had ever met. At the time (in my mid-20s), I was beginning to understand the danger of trusting every individual I came across. After a few heartbreaks, I had made "genuine" my preference, and I saw that in my husband Matthew.

Matt now and again self-identifies as being on the spectrum. He can find safety and understanding in spotting inclinations that fall somewhere on the spectrum. However, for Matt, those inclinations are more of a barrier than a disability.

For our middle son, Corbin, who is experiencing autism, it is simply a disability, impeding each element of what he can access. Corbin is 10 years old, unable to talk, and autistic. Corbin evaluates developmentally in the 12–24-month range on many examinations, and yet we know his insight is properly past that. Corbin uses a speech device; but, he requires a significant amount of support to make use of that device, and his use isn't currently enough for us to depend on the words he chooses to accurately represent what he's trying to say.

It is almost impossible to apprehend exactly what interferes with Corbin connecting with the world in the way other people do. It isn't always certainly a communication distinction—his interests, skills, strengths, dreams, and the way he comprehends and interfaces with the environment could all be considered exceptional. Some people attempt to simplify it, assuming that, "If I couldn't speak or had social tension and this happened, I might presume or feel like this." It's a disservice to Corbin to attempt to make him simpler to understand; but, it's also a disservice to pretend he's so different because, eventually, he just needs what every little boy wants: to be cherished, to be heard, and to experience the things he prefers even as he tries to keep away from the ones he dislikes. In that way, there are similarities, even though the layers, to his center, are uniquely distinct. As a society, we've taken the limits off neurodiversity and autism in a great manner. The whole lot from TV shows like "The Good Doctor" to being instructed that Bill Gates and Steve Jobs are neurodivergent has opened doorways to reduce the stigma around autism. But, what about neurodivergent children who don't match this model?

Is it helping them, or are we simply setting them up for a greater fall when we cannot regulate society's expectations and, instead of being left out or ridiculed, people start asking what their superpower is—as though each autistic baby is a savant with a hidden genius simply waiting to be discovered?

The truth is that I a lot of sleep thinking about Corbin. His disability is what it is, and we do everything we can to protect, support, and accommodate him. However, what about his potential? Can humans permit him to thrive if he's not a savant? What if he fails to learn how to speak, always has loud vocal tics, and struggles with hygiene?

Will the global community ever meet Corbin, or are they too busy seeking out Rain Man or the Good Doctor?

I respect all ranges of neurodivergence and its expression in the world. I'm satisfied that many neurodivergent humans have helped propel opportunities to people with a great mind, social, and communication variations. However is it enough?

Are we having the difficult conversations that ought to take place so Corbin can thrive inside the globe? People regularly tell me, "Corbin lives in his own world," and I have to mention that I hate hearing that as it's just not correct. Corbin is so present, and assuming he's elsewhere while he's before you definitely speaks to the extent of bias that neurodivergent humans endure each day. The hazard of the "different world theory" is that it makes it less difficult to fail to change the world.

Even as a few autistics have raised the bar and chipped away at the stigma, we have yet to witness an upward move in expectations. I recognize that an immeasurable quantity of human beings, time, cash, and services are going into schooling and caring for neurodiverse children, but we nevertheless remain in an international community of biased potential.

We to date segregate our most affected youngsters into corners of the school wherein they cannot interfere with the progress of the regular students. We still discuss tolerance, acceptance, and embracing in halls full of brilliant lighting fixtures, loud noises, crowds, and misunderstanding. We send unclear messages to those with neurodiversity. With our words, we tell them it's okay to be unique. However, we spend endless hours trying to teach them how to act like us, and the very things that appeal to us.

I accept that we are in a time where minds are beginning to open quicker than we may be able to digest all the facts coming to us. I trust that human beings now want to do and be better, and that a lot of us are desperately looking to discern how to allow our biases to leave us so we can stay in that kind of state our hearts so desire.

I consider that Corbin's future has so much potential, the ability to stay in a planet that has no bias in his direction. No bias that assumes he's doing neurological magic tricks on the inside of his hugely untapped mind, and no bias that assumes he cannot. A place where humans take a look at Corbin and believe that, until they understand him, there's no way they are able to certainly recognize his ability.

When I met my husband, I wondered, "What will this man be able to do with his life. I actually need to stay around to find out." As at the time we met, he was in his mid-20s, living with his mother, and unemployed. I do not forget that I thought, "That's stupid; he has to do ALLLLLL that matters." I believed completely that he could, and he did. He really did. I didn't understand anything concerning neurodivergence then, and I never noticed the glass ceiling for my husband. I'm a problem solver by nature, and for each challenge his differences brought up, collectively we took into consideration the possible solutions. I helped when it was within my power and prayed if I couldn't. Ultimately, he stepped into a career, a marriage, fatherhood, home ownership, and plenty of things by which society measures fulfillment.

My husband's career has spanned from being a prep cook at a chain eatery to being the Lead Quality Inspector at a Fortune 500 organization, and now the greatest job of being a stay-at-home dad, looking after our three boys.

I am not trying to talk myself up; I simply only saw all of my husband's potential due to the fact that I used to be a naive woman who went in without a predisposed notion and got to know him.

All I can ever desire for Corbin's future—in the place of work, in relationships, and in all of his endeavors, is that he has the opportunity to live beyond his unbiased potential. All I want is for people to look at him and say to themselves, "I am not familiar with Corbin. I do not know what Corbin can and might be able to do until I get closer to Corbin."

No group of people, parent, or book can tell you who Corbin is and what he's going to do or be at some point.

If you're a parent or guardian of neurotypical children, you can help by simply becoming curious and letting your children know that being distinctive is just normal.

Whenever Corbin is around other children, gets excited, becomes loud, bangs his fists on a desk, and excitedly squeals, and I hear someone say to their infant, "Corbin is happy; that's how he expresses joy. What do you do whenever you are full of joy?" I see the beginnings of a future I trust in for Corbin. Inside absolutely everyone, they keep their own potential, ever-changing based on their obstacles, society, environment, and ideas about themselves. That isn't a fixed potential, it's fluid, and we drive it with the manner with which we discuss issues around neurodiverse children. We also change it through the manner we communicate about neurodiverse children. We change it with the privileges we present to neurodiverse children, and when I talk about my desires for Corbin, I cannot achieve this without discussing my expectations for the world we live in. See, Corbin does not just live in his own world. He does not live in our world either. We all live in the world. He is as much a part of this planet as you or me. He does not visit other places. He's currently not in an alternative place where his purpose, targets, dreams and desires are met. He's ours! We're also his!

Neurodiversity inclusion begins when you start to let go of both everything you expect from a neurotypical person and the entirety of what you think you know about autism and absolutely get to learn about the individual before you."

Janaiah C. von Hassel
Mom, wife, and neurodiversity advocate

Neurodiversity

The beginning of the 21st century has witnessed another battle in the war for equal recognition: disability rights and, specifically, the autistic-led Neurodiversity Movement. This aspect of disability rights has often been overlooked, though it is critical within the context of DEI. If the goal is to build more effective and creative teams and diversity is a key factor in accomplishing that goal, then including people who are neurodiverse is essential.

The subject of Neurodiversity has a significant impact on a large segment of the population. Learning more about conscious/ unconscious biases regarding neurodiversity can help in a variety of ways. The takeaway is that it is important to value the contributions that everyone makes to society, including the neurodiverse.

The neurodiverse population has been historically undervalued. Now, many believe it is time for more acceptance and inclusion. An increasing number of people who publicly identify as neurodiverse are taking on leadership roles in companies around the world. When neurodiversity is viewed as a trait to be valued instead of a problem that needs to be solved, organizations can benefit from the unique perspectives these individuals bring to the workplace.

Neurodiversity Movement

The struggle of various groups to attain equal rights was iconic to the 20th century. Although there were many roadblocks and hurdles along the way, the century represented a move toward acceptance that previous generations may have deemed impossible. Of course, the struggle for racial equality and civil rights for the LGBTQ+ community is ongoing.

An evolving issue in the 21st century relates to disability rights overall and the Neurodiversity Movement. As it is having a significant impact on society and the modern workplace, it is vital to gain an understanding about neurodiversity and the Neurodiversity Movement.

The definition of neurodiversity is widely regarded as the state of mental fitness an individual has from a traditional societal viewpoint; a key indicator of intelligence and/or productivity. Generally, there is a lack of awareness about the inequalities and unfair treatment faced by neurodiverse people. Traditionally, society has viewed neurodiversity as a negative attribute, however the idea this is untrue has been rapidly gaining acceptance.

John Elder Robinson

The History of Neurodiversity

The notion that autism and ADHD are the end result of a natural brain variation was first presented by John Elder Robinson. Instead of a flaw that needed to be corrected, Robinson believes that the brains of neurodiverse people simply work differently. It is interesting to note how privilege and neurodiversity relate in the context of disability rights, specifically due to the superiority of the treatment-based narrative in pop culture and most educational literature.

The mainstream population is fortunate in that having shared experiences and perceptions makes society and cultures easier to navigate. People with brains that are wired differently are usually expected to conform to traditional societal expectations, which may be unrealistic. These individuals are also expected to have characteristics that go along with the diagnoses they received, along with the social perceptions that correspond with them.

In his article "Cultural Conceptions, Mental Disorders, and Social Roles: A Comparison of Germany and America," J. Marshall Townsend argues that diagnosing a man or woman with autism becomes a self-fulfilling prophecy. One reason is that anyone aware of that diagnosis will perceive the individual in a specific manner. Townsend also believed that an individual who received that diagnosis, whether consciously or unconsciously, would begin to include the traits associated with the diagnosis and its expectations.

Cultural Conceptions, Mental Disorders, and Social Roles: A Comparison of Germany and America by J. Marshall Townsend

Preconceived biases deprive people from being viewed as individuals with a valuable knowledge base and skill set to offer. Biases also limit the rights of these individuals to choose what is best for them. This is a theme that recurs throughout history, when others assign social roles and expectations. Biases have historically led to rationalizations that marginalize and oppress various groups of people. At one time or another, most minorities have been the victim of unfair and discriminatory political moves that were justified by misguided beliefs and prejudices. This is no different within the context of mental health, unfortunately.

It would be an understatement to say that people with neurodevelopmental diagnoses have been grossly mistreated over the years. For example, during the 1930s and 1940s in Nazi Germany, the authorities used selective breeding and eugenics to eliminate certain tendencies that were perceived as 'undesirable.' This was termed the T4 Initiative, a targeted attempt to 'purify' the human gene pool. It was routine for the Nazis to euthanize children and adults they had deemed 'feeble-minded,' 'mentally retarded,' and those on the autism spectrum. The Nazis hoped to apply the Aktion T-4 Venture (as it was officially called then), to dispose of people with incurable chronic illnesses, and it became the declaration of author Steve Silberman that this application served as a template with which Hitler honed his very last intention.

The Nazis even developed a sanitized, medical language for describing the atrocities they committed against disabled people. Euthanizing these individuals became known as providing "final medical assistance."

Leo Kanner

Conditions had progressed very little by the time Leo Kanner first published on the subject of the 'unique' disorder he referred to as autism. Though many at the time believed that autism was the result of poor parenting, Kanner was one of the first to note that some families had a tendency toward autism. Instead of something that developed after birth and over the years, Kanner thought of autism as an innate disorder, one that could potentially be solved through genetics. In 1943, when Kanner published his paper, Autistic Disturbances of Affective Contact, the prevailing view was that autism only applied to children who were weak-minded, moronic and/or schizophrenic. Thus, his ideas presenting autism as a syndrome were a giant leap forward at the time.

Ole Ivar Løvaas

A behaviorist named Ole Ivar Løvaas studied conditioning and brought his knowledge into the treatment of autistic individuals, a procedure he referred to as Applied Behavior Analysis (ABA). As the first individual to establish treatment interventions for those with autism, his name is synonymous with autism research. Løvaas studied autism for 40 years and co-founded the Autism Society of America.

Løvaas and his colleagues used behavior modification techniques to reduce aggressive and/or self-destructive behaviors. The techniques were also used to promote appropriate behaviors, teach autistic children how to speak in words and imitate others. Throughout his career, Løvaas used positive reinforcement to promote behaviors viewed as desirable by society and the medical community.

Unfortunately, however, in the early years, when he began his career, starting in the 1950s, Løvaas and his colleagues used aversive treatment to limit self-injurious and inappropriate behavior. This included using electric shocks, slaps and verbal admonitions to limit or eliminate these undesirable behaviors. From a modern point of view, the use of aversive treatments is highly unethical and cruel.

It is worth pointing out that Løvaas ended the use of aversive treatments. This was due to his belief that this form of treatment was ineffective over longer periods. A study Løvaas conducted in 1987 showed that 47 percent of autistic children receiving ABA treatment were able to increase their IQs by 30 points and develop typical spoken language. Although this was a sharp contrast to the control group of autistic children, in which only two percent were able to achieve the same results, many have called his methods into question. Also, the study cannot be repeated due to ethical concerns.

Løvaas has been the subject of significant controversy even though he received numerous accolades from well-established psychological associations over the course of his career. He was quoted in a 1974 Psychology Today interview, stating that, "You see, you start pretty much from scratch when you work with an autistic child. You have a person in the physical sense– they have hair, a nose, a mouth– but they are not people in the psychological sense. One way to look at the job of helping children with autism is to see it as a matter of constructing a person. You have the raw materials, but you have to build the person."

It is hard to imagine a modern scientist publicly illustrating a viewpoint so offensive. It is also difficult to imagine that the use of aversion treatments was ever viewed as acceptable in the scientific community. Speculation in any context may be fruitless and unfair; however, it is easy to see why one may believe that Løvaas' decision to discontinue the use of punishment therapy was not based on ethics. Instead, the choice was likely due to his belief this form of therapy was ineffective over the long term. When asked about his reasons for eliminating the use of aversion therapy in an interview conducted by CBS in 1994, Løvaas said that, "These people are so used to pain that they can adapt to almost any kind of aversive you give them."

Autism and Neurodiversity

The Centers for Disease Control and Prevention refers to autism spectrum disorder as a developmental disability caused by differences in the brain. It is often associated with communication problems, repetitive behaviors, restricted interests and social deficits. There are many different ways that autism can manifest in people and the severity of the symptoms associated with it can vary significantly. Not that Løvaas' assertion that autistics are incomplete people needs to be disproved, for the simple fact that no individual on Earth is qualified to make such an assertion, but it is worth pointing out that autism affects people in different ways. Also, many autistics excel in the arts and sports communities. Autistics can have a razor-like focus on the task at hand, which is a trait that many believe is a requirement for reaching the status of an expert.

The idea that there are many autistic savants is widely known. It is also widely accepted that many autistics can have a talent for remembering key details, great organizational and math skills. For these and many other reasons, many believe that autism and other developmental/learning conditions are differences that should be celebrated instead of disorders that need to be cured.

This is a central thesis of the neurodiversity movement, which is most commonly associated with autism and ADHD. Other variations in brain functionality that are being considered within the context of neurodiversity include dyslexia, bipolar disorder, epilepsy and Tourette's syndrome. Proponents of neurodiversity argue that the variations in brain function that result in autism, ADHD, and others have been around since the dawn of time, which makes them a natural aspect of the evolutionary process instead of the result of an innate disorder. Their belief is that efforts should be made towards the acceptance of these individuals as people with something to contribute, that it should be destigmatized and that accommodations should be made.

A discussion of autism would be remiss in a text such as this without mentioning the controversy surrounding the idea of neurodiversity. People who disagree with the idea of neurodiversity are often from families with an autistic that is on the severe end of the spectrum. Their belief is that autism should be treated as a disability so that treatment methods can be developed. For opponents of neurodiversity, a movement toward viewing autism as a difference in how the brain functions is unacceptable because it does not take into account the struggles faced by people on the severe end of the spectrum.

Striking a balance between the viewpoints is viewed by some as preferable. In their view, efforts should continue to be made to create and implement therapy methods that are both effective and also low in cost. Proponents of this view agree that more efforts should be made to eliminate the stigma surrounding autism and ensure that residential and commercial environments are more accommodative.

The Business Case for Neurodiversity

Neurodiverse employees might struggle to get things done in exactly the same ways that management and society expect. Whether or not these expectations are unfair may be up for debate. There is very little debate around the idea, however, that homogeneity of thought can significantly reduce the potential for innovation. As the term implies, neurodiverse people approach situations in a different way than others. This allows them to develop creative solutions and solve problems. The arts, music, science, culture and technology have all benefited significantly from individuals who are able to "think outside the box."

The business case for neurodiversity is clear. Diversity creates stronger, more effective, more innovative teams—and neurodiversity is no exception. Once a high level of diversity is attained, the employees contribute to creating a culture of respect that invites new ideas and fosters a positive environment. An estimated one in four American adults struggle with diagnosable mental disorders over their lifetimes, and one in 68 children live with autism. It's crucial to create a culture of acceptance and understanding—one that embraces those who think differently and ensures that employees can feel comfortable being who they are. Building a culture that embraces the concept of neurodiversity gives people a chance to succeed if an opportunity becomes available. Treating people with autism, dyslexia, and other neurological conditions respectfully means creating an environment that fosters their strengths, addresses their weaknesses, and provides them opportunities to contribute fully at work—just like everyone else.

Since neurodiversity refers to a range of differences in the way that people sift through information, it follows that people with neurodiversity can be visual or auditory learners. As is often the case with dyslexia, neurodiverse individuals can have many other learning preferences. Treating neurodiverse individuals as disabled is only one way to think about how they learn and function in the world. In the same way that we should avoid treating women and people of color as psychologically abnormal or unhealthy, we should avoid pathologizing neurodiverse individuals. They are not defective versions of "normal" people; their brains are simply structured differently, making them creative and innovative thinkers who can be brilliant at problem-solving.

The advantages of diversity are clear for people with neurological differences, and for their colleagues. For example, people with ADHD tend to have greater creativity and spontaneity than those without ADHD—and might even make better CEOs. Autistic workers are generally more detail oriented than other employees because they notice things others miss. And at least one study has shown that having an autistic coworker makes an office less stressful for everyone involved.

Neurodiversity is a natural phenomenon and neurodiverse individuals should not be feared or stigmatized. The neurodiversity paradigm challenges us to think about how we can accommodate people with different types of minds instead of figuring out how to eliminate the traits that some view as undesirable. An important aspect of this paradigm shift involves developing an understanding of the underlying biology behind social behavior and cognition. The knowledge base related to how the brain functions and what factors contribute to differences in behavior and cognition is continually improving. Understanding the science behind social behavior can empower people to develop effective strategies for better communication and relationships.

As previously mentioned, the term neurodiversity is most commonly associated with ADHD and autism spectrum disorder, but it also includes bipolar disorder, dyslexia, epilepsy and Tourette's syndrome. The term also encompasses other cognitive variations such as dyspraxia, depression, anxiety disorders and schizophrenia. The concept of neurodiversity can refer to individuals who are nonverbal or hyper-verbal. It can also refer to people with an exceptional skill set in the areas of memory, processing speed and/ or artistic ability. Many of these differences are not visible, like the ability to focus intently on a single task for long periods of time. Tasks that depend on many of the abilities commonly associated with neurodiversity often go unrecognized by schools and employers as valuable contributions.

Judy Singer

The term neurodiversity was coined by Judy Singer in 1998 to describe key differences in human cognitive functioning related to how people socialize, learn, regulate moods and pay attention. For proponents of neurodiversity, the term describes a natural variation in the human genome. The argument for neurodiversity is that each person with autism has his or her own way of navigating the world. In essence, it says that we are all different, but that's normal.

Singer, who is an autistic, wrote about how many previously held convictions have faded away in the face of an improving knowledge base:

> For me, the key significance of the 'Autistic Spectrum' lies in its call for and anticipation of a politics of neurological diversity, or what I want to call 'Neurodiversity.' The Neurologically Different represent a new addition to the familiar political categories of class/gender/race and will augment the insights of the social model of disability. The rise of neurodiversity takes postmodern fragmentation one step further. Just as the postmodern era sees every once too solid belief melt into air, even our most taken-for granted assumptions: that we all more or less see, feel, touch, hear, smell, and sort information, in more or less the same way, (unless visibly disabled) – are being dissolved."
>
> -Disability Discourse, Mairian Corker
> Ed., Open University Press

What Singer may not have been able to imagine when she wrote this in February of 1999, however, was how extensive the concept of neurodiversity would eventually become. With more than one billion people estimated to be living with a neurological difference worldwide and consistent increases in diagnoses of these conditions, there are now many international organizations founded on the principles of neurodiversity.

Neurodiversity is not a new concept, but it is an important one. As the knowledge base pertaining to cognitive differences evolves, it has become evident that the term encompasses more than just mental illnesses and developmental disorders.

Why Is Neurodiversity So Important at Work?

Anonymous Submission from a Leader Managing an Employee that Identifies as being Neurodiverse

After I first met my former colleague Alex he told me he had an issue writing and studying because of his dyslexia. I knew nothing about neurodiversity at that point. As his manager, I searched the internet for ways to help dyslexic workers.

It turned out to be a mistake – I used to consider his weakness. After some months, I discovered Alex has above-average competencies in reasoning and that, likely, those are associated with his dyslexia.

Everyone draws from a wealth of life experiences to form opinions and create a personal identity. Many refer to personal testimonies from individuals they admire in an effort to feel more comfortable about their own lives and experiences. The identity that people build from their gender, age, race, personal history, neurological differences, education, etc., has a significant impact on an individual's perceptions and the process by which they make decisions.

Neurodiversity describes neurological differences. Neurodiverse individuals incorporate a different perception of the world into their beliefs and decision-making. In the virtual work environment and mainly inside tech-centered businesses, there is often a need to remedy complicated issues. It is also essential to constantly innovate and be creative in the face of evolving cybersecurity and/ or artificial intelligence challenges. Having more neurodiverse individuals on staff can allow for new thoughts, more innovation and a more accommodative work environment. Neurodiverse colleagues offer a unique set of abilities. It is unfortunate that the emphasis is more commonly on the challenges experienced by neurodiverse individuals. This is likely to change in the face of a growing realization that these individuals can make a variety of positive contributions to both society and organizations.

Competitive Advantages of Neurodiversity

Neurodiverse individuals often have an array of gifts that may be essential for success in the digital age. For example, some autistics are known to have exceptional creativity, superior awareness and good judgment. Other traits that are associated with some autistics are that they tend to be systematic, and imaginative, offering unique insights and perspectives.

People with ADHD also have the potential to be highly imaginative. They can even perform better on creativity assessments than people who do not have ADHD. Though it may appear to be counterintuitive, as ADHD is often associated with hyperactivity, impulsiveness and a lack of ability to concentrate, in some cases, individuals with ADHD can sometimes have an ability to focus on a task for extremely long periods, as long as it meets their interests. This state has been termed hyperfocus, and it can have a benefit with certain types of work, sports, leisure activities, etc.

People with dyslexia have been reported to have a capacity for thinking outside the box, a talent for remembering details and telling stories, and superior artistic abilities. One study showed that 84 percent of dyslexic individuals had above average scores in reasoning, evaluating opportunities, and decision making. Their abilities are valuable when it comes to viewing issues from a broader angle and assessing conditions from more than one perspective.

People with attributes such as the ones listed above have the potential to be positively impactful to the modern workplace. It can be very difficult for many people to remain focused and ignore the seemingly constant interruptions associated with the digital age, such as emails, text messages, live chats and phone calls. Neurodiverse individuals can sometimes have a greater potential to see through these distractions and maintain their focus. Some neurodiverse individuals can also perform better when it comes to habitual tasks. Taking all of these characteristics into account, neurodiverse individuals can be a valuable team member for organizations with a variety of needs.

How to Build Neurodiverse Teams

Finding neurodiverse individuals to include on the staff is not as difficult as some may think. The challenges associated with recruitment are no different than the challenges associated with finding other individuals. And, considering the benefits that could potentially arise from building a diverse team of professionals, it is worth taking the time to overcome any challenges associated with recruitment.

The next step is to understand how differences in brain functionality manifest in neurodiverse individuals. Some may have difficulty handling multiple tasks simultaneously but excel at one specific task. Others may be extremely detail-oriented but may feel uncomfortable in social situations. Still others may have difficulty making decisions but have a talent for focusing on one task for hours at a time.

For those with an interest in building a team that includes neurodiverse individuals, it is advisable to understand the different benefits the various forms of neurodiversity can offer. When recruiting customer service representatives, for example, it could be a good idea to look for both detail-oriented people who can help customers track orders, as well as people who are more outgoing, as they may be more adept at handling on-the-spot requests and suggestions.

Real-World Example

Meet John, who is a wizard in the art of data analytics. His mathematical capabilities and talents in the area of software program development are noticeably exceptional. His CV includes two master's degrees, both of which he earned with honors. All of these traits make John an obvious candidate to be recruited by a tech organization.

Until recently, John might have been overlooked. Earlier, John found a company that had started experimenting with sourcing alternative talent. Before that, he was unemployed for over 2 years. Some other firms John had discussions with had a dire need for the skills and talent he possessed. Unfortunately, however, he was not invited to join these organizations.

After observing John in the workplace, the reasons why may start to become apparent. Although he looks nice and maintains a professional appearance, he wears headphones at all times. When people try to talk to John, he does not maintain eye contact. He leans over every 10 minutes or so to tighten his shoelaces; he finds it impossible to pay attention if they are unfastened. Once his shoelaces are tight, however, John is often able to achieve the highest productivity ratings at his company. He's hardworking and averse to taking breaks. Although his assigned workplace "buddy" has encouraged him to take a break from time to time, he doesn't enjoy them.

"John" is an autistic individual whose privacy needs to be protected. In a way, he has become a representative for individuals within the programs of pioneering agencies that have started searching for neurodiverse individuals.

John is not an anomaly or as unusual as some may think. In fact, there are many individuals who are similar to John. The prevalence of autism in the United States currently stands at around one in 42 for males and one out of 189 among females. This is based on data provided by the Centers for Disease Control and Prevention. And despite the fact that organized groups and campaigns have to this point targeted autistic individuals, it should be possible to extend recruitment practices to those who with dyspraxia (a neurologically based physical disorder), dyslexia, ADHD, social anxiety problems, and various other situations. Some individuals with these diagnoses have better-than-average capabilities. A number of studies show that some individuals with autism and dyslexia can have unique talents in pattern recognition, remembrance, or mathematics. In many cases, however, these individuals do not match the profiles sought for by potential employers.

The tech industry is leading the way in the shift toward creating more neurodiverse workplaces. In 2015, Google revealed they have hired autistic people to work at the company. Microsoft has also hired employees with autism and has created a resource website for managers at other companies to find people with autism.

The two companies use very different methods for hiring workers on the spectrum. Google is open to hiring anyone on the spectrum and does not require any sort of pre-employment testing. Google says its interviewers are trained to look for certain qualities in their prospective employees, such as self-awareness and the ability to communicate. They are also trained to identify whether or not an individual's communication style is similar to that of an average person.

Microsoft, on the other hand, uses an affirmative action approach and hires based on pre-employment testing. This testing focuses on workability, skill assessment, and performance within team projects. Microsoft reports that many of the neurodiverse individuals in the company become "top performers" because they excel in isolation, which is something that is typically required of software engineers.

Company representatives that are interested in trying to create a more inclusive workplace should understand there are many issues to be aware of and research. Organizations seeking to be more inclusive of neurodiverse workers should first evaluate whether or not the company has the resources to make it happen. If so, are there assessment tools available to determine whether the process is working?

If not, are the necessary resources available to hire new people and train them? Are the proposed work roles aligned with corporate goals? Does the team have the capacity or flexibility to take on new projects? It is also worth pointing out that there could be turnover if the project isn't successful, so everyone in the organization should be prepared for this, especially those in leadership roles.

Is there a role for neurodiverse workers in the organization? If so, what would that role look like? How would these individuals be supported in their work? Providing neurodiverse workers with access to mentors who can help them navigate the workplace could be an effective way to ensure they are successful.

How will neurodiverse workers fit in with the teams that have already been established in the workplace? Will they be working with average people or other neurodiverse workers? There is evidence that neurodiverse teams are more creative and innovative than non-neurodiverse teams. Having an understanding of neurodiversity and developing necessary recruitment practices are essential if the goal is creating such teams.

While it may not be possible to create a team that entirely consists of neurodiverse individuals, it is possible to create a neurodiverse team with members whose different neurological backgrounds contribute unique perspectives and knowledge. There are numerous ways that employers can be more inclusive of neurodiversity in the workplace. Some of these strategies may not be immediately obvious, and many will require a shift in the mindset of both managers and employees.

To build a team of neurodiverse individuals, here are some key steps to remember:

- The recruitment process should be tailored to candidates with disabilities, particularly those that are invisible

- Ensure all recruitment materials, interview processes, and assessment centers are accessible to all applicants at all stages of the recruitment process
- Consider using the services of an access consultant or other specialist with experience in disability to ensure the organization is compliant with the ADA
- Encourage managers to have an open mind when interviewing candidates

Everyone involved with the recruitment process should be aware that some people may have specific learning difficulties, such as dyslexia or dyspraxia. These difficulties may affect how they answer questions and perform tasks in interviews. If a candidate is invited to an interview, it is not advisable to reject that individual because of a hidden (or observable) disability.

The workplace is changing. New legislation and a greater understanding of mental illness are supporting efforts to make workplaces more accessible. If the goal is to improve the standard of living for people with autism, workplaces need to be more accepting of neurodiverse individuals.

In the UK today, 1 in 100 people have Autism Spectrum Disorder (ASD), yet fewer than 50 percent are in full-time paid employment. Some studies suggest that up to 80 percent of adults with ASD are unemployed or underemployed. Only 14 percent work full time.

There is also a disparity between rates of unemployment and underemployment for autistic people, depending on whether they are educated. For example, 48 percent of autistic students with no qualifications are unemployed. For those who have completed higher education, only 15 percent are unemployed.

The causes of underrepresentation in employment among autistic people are complex. It is not always clear whether this is a result of discrimination or the effect of other factors, such as a lack of awareness or support from employers. Other potential hurdles that could potentially result in underrepresentation include difficulties with social skills or self-presentation, different interests from their colleagues, and problems with communication in the workplace.

Supporting Neurodiversity in the Workplace

Many organizations have a traditional one-way communication style, where messages are sent from management down to the employees, with little room for feedback from employees in the other direction. In this type of environment, employees are expected to work within strict parameters that are set by managers and supervisors.

This model can put enormous pressure on people who are neurodivergent in some way. Many autistics find it difficult to sit at a desk all day and have forced interactions with coworkers. Some autistics may find it preferable to work independently and not within the context of a team. The job roles and tasks that are expected of autistic individuals might not be problematic, but the attitude toward neurodiverse employees can sometimes result in a very harsh and difficult work environment.

To provide support for neurodiverse individuals, the organization should understand the challenges faced by these individuals and develop training programs for their fellow staff members. Training staff members on autism and related conditions can help them to understand what it means to have these conditions, as well as how to provide their colleagues with the support they need to be successful. Having the necessary training in place can also help to educate individuals about whether or not a particular industry, job or business is a good place for autistic individuals.

There is a business case for creating a culture in which neurodiversity is accepted and welcomed. Having consistent "brain breaks," where employees acknowledge their divergent experiences by sharing something quirky they've learned, an anecdote or something that made them laugh could be a good idea. Creating a comfortable work environment can also involve providing a space where individuals can rest, relax and recharge.

Case Study

The Aviva organization provides 18 million customers with essential products. This is partly achieved as a result of having a diverse workforce. The approach that Aviva had in 2019 was centered on two primary objectives: supporting existing team members who are neurodiverse, and connecting with the community to recruit new team members who are neurodiverse.

As a result of this approach, Aviva has become a leader in neurodiverse recruitment/retention practices. Aviva implemented one of the most innovative and inclusive records technological capability recruitment packages, attracting, sourcing and recruiting new employees. Many are hoping this paves the way for comparable initiatives, both in conjunction with Aviva and across all industries.

Neurodiversity as a concept has galvanized and inspired neurodiverse individuals worldwide. A positive aspect of the movement is that it has inspired some individuals to break free from stigmas and rise above societal expectations concerning their potential. Autism has been portrayed as a health crisis of epidemic proportions by the mainstream media and this interpretation leaves little room for competing views. While the intentions of most people may be good and the cure-and-crisis narrative may be effective as far as keeping people interested in the topic, it does not help to eliminate the stigma surrounding neurodiverse individuals or move society toward an increasing level of acceptance.

The neurodiversity movement has guided society to more acceptance, empowered neurodiverse individuals to rise above preconceived notions resulting from their diagnoses, and inspired organizations to hire individuals they may not have considered otherwise. A positive outcome of the movement is that neurodiverse individuals are being valued for their potential to make a contribution. The case for neurodiverse recruitment policies is especially compelling given the shortage of skilled workers that an increasing number of industries are experiencing. For example, the European Union is facing a scarcity of 800,000 IT workers in 2021. Businesses that rely heavily on statistics analyses and IT will be negatively impacted if recruitment practices are not updated to be more inclusive.

7

Gender Disparities

*Women belong in all places where decisions are being
made. It shouldn't be that women are the exception.*
—Ruth Bader Ginsburg

A Brief History of Gender Disparities

Women have been fighting for equal rights since the United States was formed in various ways. One of the most notable struggles, of course, was the path leading up to the suffrage movement. Before the passing of the 19th Amendment on August 18, 1920, women were not allowed to vote. It is worth pointing out, however, that certain states allowed women to vote as early as 1866. Black men were not allowed to vote until 1870, but that changed as a result of the 15th Amendment. While a significant milestone, the 19th Amendment did not grant full voting rights for all women. As a result of local laws, taxes and other restrictions, the right to vote for non-white women was not attained until 40 years later.

The civil rights movement drew attention to a variety of marginalized groups, including women. These groups had not been equally protected under the law. Women continued to face many barriers and discrimination. It was not until 1869 until a woman, Arabella Mansfield, became the first practicing attorney in the United States. Also, it was not until the 1970s that no-fault divorce became legally permissible, and this had vast implications for women. The workplace "glass ceiling" still exists. Women continue to combat workplace discrimination and pay inequities. A clear example of this is that the United States does not have comprehensive maternity leave and job security for women. Women attain higher education levels than men; they represent 50 percent of the workforce and occupy almost 20 percent of elected positions in the US (2020).

A century has passed since women were given the right to vote. The victory was preceded by decades of protest and conflict. The amendment was first introduced in Congress nearly half of a century earlier, in 1878. It was not until 1918 that President Woodrow Wilson changed his position in support of the amendment.

100 Years after the 19ᵗʰ Amendment

There are around 7.8 billion people on Earth and women are the majority. This can make it surprising to learn that gender inequality persists. Women account for over 47 percent of the global workforce and maintain over half of all the jobs inside the US. Experts predict an upward trend of women in the workplace, and a downtrend in the number of men.

The idea that women are happier when they are not involved in the workforce holds very little merit. The employment gap between men and women is not due to the fact that women want to stay home. In fact, nearly 70 percent of women have indicated that they would choose a paying job in place of staying in the home full time. Nevertheless, the gender employment gap has continued.

Over half of all jobs that require a university degree are held by women. Education is associated with earnings and this point is essential for women. Statistics show that women are surpassing men by 0.2 percent in the levels of education they have attained. Over the past 10 years, women acquired a total of 57 percent of all bachelor's degrees, 59 percent of all master's degrees, and 53 percent of all PhDs.

In 2019, the Fortune 500 listing found that 33 women were more effective at leading large companies than their male counterparts. Additionally, the S&P 500 Index indicates that during 2019, women accounted for 26 percent of board directors.

What does this mean?

Economic sectors that are traditionally associated with women are gaining a larger share of female employees than others. There have always been larger numbers of women in economic sectors such as schooling and healthcare. The percentage of female workers that could be classified as managers or leaders was only found to be around 27 percent in one study.

Women from diverse cultural backgrounds typically receive less pay for the same work. Also, it is more difficult for women to rise above the level of middle management than men. One study showed that 55 percent of women in senior roles reported being sexually harassed. A third of women in the corporate world reported being victims of sexual harassment, with 48 percent of that group identifying as being part of the LGBTQIA+ community. Around 64 percent of women said they have dealt with micro-aggressions at work, where they felt their opinions and ideas were being overlooked.

The gender pay gap is common worldwide. One study showed that women earn 16 percent less than men per hour and 22 percent less on a monthly basis. Another study illustrated the idea that gender discrimination is an ongoing problem, as it showed that, for every dollar earn by men, women only earn $0.82.

How many CEOs are women?

At the time of this writing, the Fortune 500 listing showed that only 33 women have the top role in major international organizations. Additionally, the S&P 500 Index suggests that, in 2019, the number of women with positions on the board of directors for major companies was only 26 percent.

Why are female employees so important?

Recent studies show that women have a positive impact on employee retention and engagement. Fortune 500 corporations with large numbers of women holding executive positions report higher levels of overall performance relative to competitors with smaller numbers of women on their boards.

According to several studies, the global workforce is comprised of around 47 percent women. It is also worth noting that 50.2 percent of college-educated workers are women. There are many other key takeaways that a number of studies have made clear in regard to female workers, including:

- Around 27 percent of managers and leaders are women
- Over 60 percent of women think motherhood would disrupt their career
- In the past 20 years, the number of female software engineers has hovered around two percent
- Around 42 percent of women have reported discrimination at work due to gender

- Nearly 50 percent of female employees have entry-level roles
- Work-life balance is a concern for 72 percent of female employees

Women have made substantial leaps forward over the past few centuries as workers, educators, writers, artists, leaders and entrepreneurs. Their ability to climb the ranks and shatter glass ceilings may have been unthinkable to previous generations.

Image: World Economic Forum - Gender Gap Report 2020 World Economic Forum - Global Gender Gap Report 2020

Similarly, a century after being granted the right to vote, women continue to be underrepresented in political leadership roles.

World Economic Forum - Global Gender Gap Report 2020

Warriors of the Movement

There are so many women throughout history who have made a positive impact on advancing women's rights. It was difficult to choose a few to highlight and this is by no means a complete list. The following are highly influential female leaders who made positive contributions to the human rights movement.

Mary Seacole - November 1805–May 1881

Until recently, when my eight-year-old daughter chose to do a report on her at school, I had never heard of Mary Seacole. Seacole

was an international hero, a Jamaican woman of mixed race who selflessly treated wounded soldiers. She was not only able to save many human lives, but her bravery and courage also resulted in many positive strides against gender bias. Seacole was a daring adventurer of the 19th century who was awarded the Order of Merit posthumously by the Jamaican government and celebrated as a "Black Briton" in the United Kingdom.

Mary Jane Seacole was born in Kingston, Jamaica. Her father, James Grant, was a Scottish lieutenant in the British Army. Seacole called her Creole mother an "admirable doctress," meaning a user of conventional herbal remedies. Seacole and her mother ran a boarding house for officers in Kingston and looked after lodgers who had been unwell. She recanted the teachings of her mother as well as what she learned about medicine from the doctors who stayed in their boarding house in her autobiography, The Wonderful Adventures of Mrs. Seacole.

In the text, Seacole wrote that she was proud her heritage consisted of both Jamaican and Scottish roots: "I am a Creole, and have good Scots blood coursing through my veins. My father was a soldier of an old Scottish family." Seacole focused on illustrating the amount of vigor and enthusiasm she had in her professional life in an effort to distance herself from an unfortunate stereotype that existed at the time regarding the work ethic of those with Creole roots.

Seacole spent an extensive amount of time in England as a teenager. She also visited the Bahamas, Haiti, and Cuba, where she purchased items to sell in Kingston. In 1836, she married Edwin Seacole. It has been reported that Edwin was an illegitimate son of Admiral Lord Nelson, though Mary referred to him as Nelson's godson in her will. In 1843, the boarding house she ran with her mother, Blundell Hall, was destroyed in a fire. After rebuilding the boarding house that would become New Blundell Hall, Seacole lost her mother and her husband, in 1844.

Seacole turned her misfortune into strength, treating numerous European military visitors while running the new boarding house. She treated sufferers of a cholera epidemic in Kingston in 1850, "receiving many recommendations as to its remedy which afterwards I discovered precious." Seacole then traveled to Cruces, Panama, to visit her half-brother Edward. He had opened the Independent Hotel to serve prospectors traveling in between the east and west coasts of the US searching for gold.

The cholera epidemic arrived in Panama shortly after Seacole's arrival there. She was able to successfully treat the first victim, which helped to establish her credibility as a medical practitioner. This resulted in numerous sick individuals turning to Seacole for assistance, though she was only moderately successful. The remedies she used included mustard emetics, heat poultices, mustard plasters on the belly and the lower back, sugars of lead, mercury chloride and rehydration. Although common at the time, these treatments are now known to be harmful and Seacole had very little help from other medical professionals, thus, the epidemic went on unabated. When it was nearly over, she also fell with the disease, but was able to recover after a few weeks.

Seacole was honest about the mistakes she had made in treating people and how a few treatments she had used made her "shudder" after learning more about medicine. From Panama, Seacole traveled to Gorgona, a Columbian island in the Pacific Ocean. She ran a hotel for women there for a short time before returning to Kingston in 1853. On a return trip to Panama to tie up some loose ends associated with her business, Seacole read about the Crimean War, which had begun to escalate.

The war began when Russia invaded territory that was controlled by the Ottoman Empire. The conflict was partially based on an argument over how Christians in Palestine, which was controlled by the Ottoman Empire, should be treated. It was also based on years of remaining hostilities and bad feelings that had resulted from the Russo-Turkish Wars, a series of 12 wars between the two countries. The Crimean peninsula is a valuable strategic position for a variety of reasons. This is partially why Britain and France decided to join the conflict, to help preserve the balance of power in the area and ensure the Ottoman Empire would be able to maintain control over Crimea.

These allied nations were later joined by the Italian Kingdom of Sardinia in the fight against Russia, which asked for peace after an unsuccessful, 11-month long defense of Sevastopol.

Seacole's association with the war began when she learned that many of the soldiers she had treated in Jamaica were going to be deployed in the fight. This motivated her to travel to England, along with a need to take care of some investments. Once there, she tried to join a contingent of nurses in an effort to help. Seacole also applied to several governmental bodies and the Crimean Fund, which had been funded by public donations, to sponsor her travel to the Crimea, but she was consistently rebuffed. After considering that she provided several examples of her medical abilities, this led her to believe that she was being rejected due to the color of her skin. Seacole wondered in her autobiography if England had been influenced by American racial prejudices: "Was it possible that American prejudices against colour had some root here? Did these ladies shrink from accepting my aid because my blood flowed beneath a somewhat duskier skin than theirs?"

Unable to gain acceptance into the nursing contingent or sponsorship from the Crimean Fund, Seacole decided to use her own money to make the trip. She partnered with an old friend, Thomas Day, to open the British Hotel. It was originally envisioned as a boarding house and a place for soldiers to recover, similar to Blundell Hall, but a friend advised the partners to focus on food and beverage, as the soldiers had other places available to recuperate. The hotel was located at a place she called Spring Hill, in present day Ukraine and built out of salvaged materials, such as old packing cases, driftwood, discarded metal, doors and windows.

Seacole gathered a variety of supplies to sell to the troops, cooked meals for service in-house and catered meals, often for spectators of the battles. She also visited the troops to sell them supplies. It was Seacole's focus on nursing the sick and dying, however, which earned her acclaim and the moniker "Mother Seacole." Numerous firsthand accounts speak to her selflessness and commitment to comfort the soldiers through providing medical assistance. Seacole also famously brewed hot tea to provide to the soldiers at her own expense, sometimes serving over 200 a day.

To care for the wounded, sick and dying, Seacole typically carried medical supplies with her, including bandages, needles and thread. She was one of the first individuals to enter Sevastopol after it fell and, once there, provided refreshments to many injured Russian soldiers. After the war ended, the store was left with an inventory glut and Seacole experienced financial hardship. She returned to England in poor financial shape though she made the lives of many soldiers richer through her contributions. A number of accounts illustrate that Seacole, while operating her store, was able to provide care for numerous sick individuals, which cemented her reputation as a selfless, compassionate person.

Though she was forced to declare bankruptcy, Seacole benefited from a variety of fundraising efforts. These were led by some elite British friends including Major General Lord Rokeby and Lord George Paget, who were both involved in the Crimean War, Prince Edward and the Duke of Wellington. Along with the sale of her autobiography, the first of its kind written in England by a black woman, this helped to improve Seacole's financial position.

The Wonderful Adventures of Mrs. Mary Seacole in Many Lands

In her lifetime, Seacole was portrayed in an honorary bust sporting medals of the highest distinction for her service, from England, France, Turkey and Sardinia. It has even been reported that Russia also honored her with a medal, although there are no formal records indicating that she was awarded any medals. Numerous buildings were named after Seacole in Jamaica, starting in the 1950s. In 1990, Jamaica honored Seacole with the Order of Merit, the country's fourth-highest honor. Many public institutions and buildings in England have been named in her honor since then, and her life is now a part of the British educational curriculum.

Caroline King, PhD

Recovered Portrait of Mary Seacole

> *Unless I am allowed to tell the story of my life*
> *in my own way, I cannot tell it at all.*
>
> \- Mary Seacole

Ruth Bader Ginsburg
(March 15, 1933–September 18, 2020)

Few have done more to advance the cause of women's rights than Ruth Bader Ginsburg. A native of Brooklyn, New York, Ginsburg served on the Supreme Court from 1993 to 2020. She was the second female to serve on the Court and the first woman of Jewish descent.

Ginsburg earned a bachelor's degree from Cornell University, where she met her husband, Martin Ginsburg. They were married shortly after graduation and moved to Oklahoma soon after, as Martin Ginsburg was a member of the US Army Reserve. This was during the Korean War and he was called into active duty. While there, Ruth Bader Ginsburg worked in an office of the Social Security Administration. She got pregnant when she was working there and was subsequently demoted as a result.

The couple had their first baby shortly before Ruth Bader Ginsburg entered Harvard Law School, where she was one of nine females out of a class of approximately 500 men. When she was there, the dean reportedly asked the female students, "Why are you at Harvard Law School, taking the place of a man?"

This likely made the decision easier to follow her husband when he was offered a job in New York City. Eventually graduating from Columbia Law School, where she was one of the top in her class, Ginsburg was the first woman to be a part of two law reviews, the Harvard Law Review and the Columbia Law Review. Although she had an impeccable academic record, Ginsburg struggled to find work in the legal field and was rejected from a high-profile clerkship because of her gender.

Fortunately, one of Ginsburg's professors from Columbia

recommended her to Judge Edmund Palmieri of the US District Court for the Southern District of New York, and he relented. After working as a clerk for two years, she accepted a role at the Columbia Law School Project on International Procedure, initially working as a research associate before rising to the position of associate director. It was during this time she co-wrote a book with Anders Bruzelius on Swedish civil procedure. To write the book, Ginsburg learned Swedish and spent an extensive amount of time conducting research at Lund University in Sweden. The experience had a formative impact on her professional development, as the Bruzelius' family was heavily involved in the legal field and the society there had a much more egalitarian view pertaining to the role and potential of women.

In 1963, Ginsburg accepted a position at Rutgers Law School as a professor. There, she was told that she would receive less pay than her male counterparts. The justification Ginsburg received for this action was that her husband already had a good job. A development such as this is hard to imagine today and that is partially a result of the impact Ginsburg had in the cause to advance women's rights over the course of her career. In spite of this, Ginsburg worked at Rutgers as a professor until 1972.

Starting in 1972, Ginsburg worked at Columbia Law School as a professor, eventually becoming the first woman to ever earn tenure there. She also co-wrote the first law school casebook outlining discrimination based on sex. In the same year, Ginsburg began working with the American Civil Liberties Union (ACLU), where she partnered with a colleague to found the Women's Rights Project. As general counsel and director of the project, Ginsburg worked alongside the ACLU, taking part in over 300 cases with gender discrimination issues. With an emphasis on strategy and the idea that it might be more feasible to tackle individual statutes on a step-by-step basis, rather than seeking to end all discriminatory practices simultaneously, she argued six cases in front of the Supreme Court between 1973 and 1976.

In several cases, Ginsburg selected male plaintiffs in an effort to demonstrate that gender-based discrimination was negatively impactful to both men and women. One example is provided by the case of Moritz v. Commissioner from 1972, in which she successfully argued for a male plaintiff who was denied a tax deduction for being a caregiver as a result of his gender. In 1973, Ginsburg took on the case of a female member of the Armed Forces who wanted to claim a housing allowance for her husband. A statute was making it harder for female service members to claim a housing allowance than male service members; she was able to show that the statute treated women as inferior and won the case.

In a similar case, Ginsburg argued on behalf of a widower who had been denied survivor benefits by the Social Security Administration. The organization allowed for special benefits to be provided to widows but not for widowers. Ginsburg was able to show this was a clear example of gender-based discrimination. She was also able to show, in a separate case, that jury duty should not be optional for women and required for men, as this represented unequal treatment under the law.

By working within the law and pursuing small, realistic victories instead of making broad statements, issuing public complaints or demonizing those in power, Ginsburg was able to make significant positive strides in the cause for women's rights. This is partially why many viewed her as a moderate consensus-builder in her early career. In the second half of her career, however, Ginsburg would become more outspoken, writing fiery dissents and serving as the leader of the liberal justices on the Supreme Court.

In response to a backlog of federal cases, a law was passed in 1978 to increase the number of judges. Ginsburg, who at the time was developing a written account of her legal career as a fellow at Stanford University, filled out a questionnaire for potential nominees. With the support of her husband, who was working behind the scenes to illustrate her potential as a judge, she was nominated to the US Court of Appeals for the District of Columbia Circuit by then-President Jimmy Carter and approved by the Senate a few months later.

While serving on the DC Circuit, Ginsburg earned a reputation for her ability to reach across party lines and find common ground with her colleagues. She developed beneficial relationships with conservatives such as Robert Bork and Antonin Scalia, the latter of which would last for many years, and served until 1993 when she became a Supreme Court justice.

It was partially due to the efforts of former US Attorney General Janet Reno and former Republican Senator Orrin Hatch that Ginsburg entered the radar of President Bill Clinton, who nominated her to the Supreme Court. After a number of judicial hearings, in which she refused to answer a number of questions about her views, explaining that she may have to vote on them at some point, she was confirmed by the Senate in a 96-3 vote in August of 1993.

Similar to her work in the 1970s with the ACLU, Ginsburg has been portrayed as a consensus builder with a focus on making small, achievable strides in her early years on the Supreme Court. After Sandra Day O'Connor retired in 2006, Ginsburg became the only female on the Court. It was during this time that she first began reading dissents from the bench if she was in disagreement with the majority opinion. When John Paul Stevens retired in 2010, Ginsburg became the highest-ranking liberal on the Court, a leadership role that allowed her to have lower ranking justices write dissenting opinions when necessary.

In 1996, Ginsburg outlined the opinion of the Court in a case involving Virginia Military Institute (VMI). At the time, VMI was a male-only institution. It had floated the idea of creating a separate, women-only institution, however, Ginsburg found this idea too similar to discriminatory, separate but equal practices and policies. She wrote that, "Generalizations about 'the way women are,' estimates of what is appropriate for most women, no longer justify denying opportunity to women whose talent and capacity place them outside the average description." Chief Justice William Rehnquist, a conservative, agreed with Ginsburg and the male-only admissions policy was abolished.

There were many other cases in which Ginsburg made positive strides in the push for equality and women's rights. In the case of Ledbetter v. Goodyear in 2007, Ginsburg dissented from the majority opinion, writing in favor of equal pay and asking Congress to reverse the decision of the Court. She is partially credited for President Barack Obama signing the Lilly Ledbetter Fair Pay Act into law in 2008, making it easier to win claims based on pay discrimination.

Ginsburg was also a famous supporter of abortion rights. In a dissent from the majority opinion in a case in 2007, Gonzales v. Carhart, she wrote in opposition to the belief of the majority that it would be permissible to defer to legislative findings regarding the safety of partial birth abortions for women. In a similar case in 2016 that eliminated portions of a law in Texas that regulated abortion providers, Ginsburg wrote that the true goal of the former legislation was not based on an effort to protect the health and safety of women but instead to limit their access to abortions.

During her time on the Court, Ginsburg helped to protect citizens from unfair search and seizure. In a separate case, she argued that improperly collected evidence should be suppressed as a method of making police accountable for mistakes and preserve civil rights. Ginsburg was also an avid supporter of voting rights and affirmative action, though she did believe that affirmative action practices would have an end point. She also wrote in concurrence with a majority opinion that mental illness is a form of disability and made positive steps for the environmental movement by writing a majority opinion in 2000 allowing individuals from affected communities to seek restitutions against industrial polluters.

Although Ginsburg tended to vote in agreement with liberal viewpoints, she had positive relationships with several conservative judges. She and conservative Justice Antonin Scalia famously bonded over their shared love of opera and she thought of him as her closest Supreme Court colleague. The two often dined together and even appeared in an opera, Ariadne auf Naxos, together on two occasions. It was also not uncommon for Ginsburg to praise the work of her colleague William Rehnquist.

Marty and Ruth

Ruth Bader Ginsburg and Martin "Marty" Ginsburg were married for 56 years and had two children. Marty was initially diagnosed with cancer after the birth of their daughter in 1955 and eventually passed away from it in 2010 just after their anniversary. The pair famously spoke about the importance of having a shared earning/shared parenting marriage, in which both partners share equal responsibility for generating household income, taking care of children and maintaining the house, as well as having equal time for recreation.

Ruth Bader Ginsburg and Marty Ginsburg. Justice Ginsburg described her husband as "the only young man I dated who cared that I had a brain."

At the time when they were married, it was a somewhat groundbreaking idea for a husband to support the career of his wife. As Justice Ginsburg wrote, "I betray no secret in reporting that, without him (Marty), I would not have gained a seat on the Supreme Court." This takes nothing away from the many years of hard work that resulted in Justice Ginsburg earning a seat on the Supreme Court. Marty believed in the importance of Ruth's work and made

113

concerted efforts, both in public and behind the scenes, to ensure she had the support she needed to be successful. Marty was a leading tax attorney from an internationally prominent firm at the time his wife was appointed to the DC circuit. It has been reported that Marty already wanted to leave the firm, yet it is still worth pointing out, since it was a fairly unheard-of practice at the time, that he made the move to DC to support his wife, accepting a professorship at Georgetown University. After he passed away, Justice Ginsburg observed a letter he had written to her which read, "What a treat it's been to observe you progress to the very pinnacle."

The Notorious RBG

As a result of her growing outspokenness and passionate dissents in support of equal rights, Ginsburg was honored with the moniker The Notorious RBG, a reference to deceased rap star The Notorious BIG. This was also due to the work of a blogger, Shana Knizhnik, who partnered with a reporter to convert her blog about Ginsburg into a best-selling book, Notorious RBG: The Life and Times of Ruth Bader Ginsburg. Though some progressives have criticized her, stating that her voting record was much more moderate than other justices, she has been immortalized as a cultural icon in the movement toward equal rights. It is possible to find an array of pop culture items and merchandise sporting the RBG moniker and Ginsburg famously admitted to having a large inventory of Notorious RBG t-shirts, which she liked to gift to family and friends.

Ginsburg served on the Supreme Court for 27 years and rarely took time off, even while enduring several bouts with cancer.

Legal scholars pushed her to resign when President Obama was in office and the potential to appoint a Democratic candidate was higher, but she refused and received criticism as a result. In an interview in 2016, Ginsburg expressed dismay at the chance that Republican candidate Donald Trump might be elected president—a declaration that would become extensively criticized as no longer aligned with the courtroom's tradition of staying out of politics. She later stated that she regretted making the observation. Trump's electoral victory renewed the complaint that Ginsburg should have retired when Obama was president, as Trump was able to appoint a conservative to the Court in 2020 after she passed away at the age of 87. Complications from pancreatic cancer were the culprit. Thousands of mourners waited in line to view Ginsburg's casket, on display in the West portico of the Court. The casket was relocated after two days to the Capitol where Ginsburg lay in state, becoming the first female and the first person of Jewish descent to do so.

State of the Union since 2009.

Reverend Anna Pauline "Pauli" Murray

Anne Pauline Murray was born on November 20, 1910 in Baltimore Maryland, the fourth of six children born to Agnes Fitzgerald and William Murray. When Murray was three, her mother died from a massive cerebral hemorrhage. Murray's father—who was a graduate of Howard University, a teacher and later, a principal in the Baltimore School District, was left to raise six children on his own. Subsequently, Murray was sent to live with two of her maternal aunts in North Carolina. Three years later, her father was committed to the Crownsville State Hospital for the Negro Insane. In 1922, William was beaten and killed by a white guard. Murray stated this event was "the most significant fact of my childhood."

Reverend Anna Pauline "Pauli" Murray
(November 20, 1910–July 1, 1985)

After graduating high school at 15, Murray was qualified to attend any top university. Murray refused to apply to the North Carolina College for Negroes because of not wanting to be further confined by segregation. Murray set her sights on Columbia University, but the school did not admit women. *Murray instead attended Hunter College in New York City, at the time an all-women's school. While at Hunter, she moved into the Harlem YWCA. While in Harlem, Murray became friends with Langston Hughes, met W.E.B. DuBois, heard Mary McLeod Bethune speak, and saw Duke Ellington and Cab Calloway perform at the Apollo Theatre. Murray also began writing poetry, getting published in various magazines, including The Crisis, a publication of the NAACP.*

In the 1930s Murray came to terms with her gender identity. Murray changed her birth name from "Anne Pauline" to "Pauli." Murray also began looking for gender-affirming treatments, including hormone therapy, but was denied. In 1938, Murray moved back to North Carolina. Murray applied to the graduate program in sociology at UNC-Chapel Hill, but was denied entry due to race. Murray fought for the right to attend due to family connections. Two of Murray's white, slave-owning ancestors had attended UNC and another served on the Board of Trustees. In 1940, Murray and a friend were arrested and sent to jail for refusing to move to the back of the bus during an interstate trip from New York to North Carolina.

Back in New York, Murray began fundraising for the Workers Defense League. Working on behalf of an imprisoned sharecropper, Murray wrote a letter to President Roosevelt accusing him of caring more about Fascism abroad than racism at home. While FDR did not respond to the letter, his wife Eleanor Roosevelt did, and the two began a friendship. As part of the effort, Murray also gave a speech in Richmond that was heard by both Thurgood Marshall and Howard Law Professor Leon Ransom. Ransom approached Murray after the speech and encouraged her to apply to Howard Law School promising a scholarship if they got in. Murray did and enrolled with the single-minded intention of destroying Jim Crow. While at Howard, Murray thrived. In a 1944 paper s/he wrote, Murray proposed challenging the "separate" part of the Plessy vs. Ferguson (1896) Supreme Court decision as a violation of the 13th and 14th Amendments; this argument eventually formed the basis for the Brown vs. Board of Education (1954) case. The professor for whom Murray wrote the paper was on the team arguing segregation in education was a constitutional violation. While at Howard, Murray also organized sit-ins in Washington D.C. to desegregate restaurants and urged classmates to go south to fight for civil rights.

Murray was the only woman at Howard Law School at the time and graduated at the top of her class in 1944. It was customary then for Howard's top law school grad to automatically receive a fellowship, but she was denied due to her gender (Harvard did not admit women). Opting instead for the University of California Berkeley's School of Law, she earned a master's degree and wrote "The Right to Equal Opportunity in Employment" as her thesis, a work that was published in the school's prestigious California Law Review. Murray famously coined the phrase "Jane Crow" discrimination, referring to discrimination based on gender and race. Drawing from numerous firsthand experiences, she wrote about Jane Crow on several occasions and frequently delivered public speeches on the topic.

After graduating from Berkeley, Murray returned to NYC and scraped by on low-paying odd jobs. In 1950, she published States' Laws on Race and Color, an assessment and criticism of the states' use of segregation laws nationwide. The ACLU began distributing copies of the book to law libraries, HBCUs, and human-rights organizations. Thurgood Marshall kept stacks of it around the NAACP office and referred to it as "the bible" of the civil rights movement. In the work, Murray advised civil rights attorneys to point out that segregation laws were unconstitutional instead of working to show that the separate but equal doctrine did not result in equal facilities for non-whites. It has been noted that her approach was essential the success of Brown vs. Board of Education.

In 1956, Murray became the first Black female associate attorney at Paul, Weiss, a prestigious law firm in New York. She worked there for four years and it was there she first met Ruth Bader Ginsburg, who was there for a summer. Later, when Ginsburg argued that women should receive equal protection under the law in Reed v. Reed in 1971, she honored Murray as a co-author in the legal brief, as her ideas had been inspirational. Murray worked closely with civil rights leaders, but frequently criticized them for the way they sidelined women in the movement.

In 1965, Murray became the first African American to earn a doctorate in Juridical Science from Yale Law School. In 1966, Murray was one of the twelve founders of the National Organization for Women (NOW). But after feeling NOW sidelined women of color, Murray left the organization and joined the Equal Employment Opportunity Commission (EEOC). In 1968, Murray received a tenure-track job teaching American Studies at Brandeis University, where she launched courses on both African-American and women's studies. She left in 1973 to break one more barrier. In 1977, Murray became the first African American woman in the United States to become an Episcopal priest. Murray administered her first Eucharist at the Chapel of the Cross on Franklin Street in Chapel Hill; the church is steps away from UNC's campus—a school that had denied Murray entry based on their race. Pauli Murray died of cancer in Pittsburgh on July 1, 1985. Due to Murray's dogged work and courage, she is regarded as one of the most important social justice advocates of the 20ᵗʰ century.

Murray is referred to here as a 'she' to acknowledge the fact that the term transgender did not exist in her time and the idea that assigning pronouns posthumously may be beyond the scope of this work. Several scholars have categorized her as a transgender man, which may be accurate from a modern viewpoint, as she referred to herself as having an urge that motivated her to behave as a man would potentially behave if attracted to a woman.

8

LGBTQIA+

History of the Movement

In the 1960s, homosexuality was listed as a mental illness by the American Psychiatric Association. This classification resulted in people losing employment if they were suspected of being a homosexual. After World War II, the US government viewed homosexuality as an act of perversion and not "normal." Law enforcement kept lists of suspected homosexuals and tracked their movements. Conducting sweeps of neighborhoods to rid them of homosexuals was a routine practice. In 1965, the gay rights organization the Mattachine Society campaigned to stop the entrapment.

The homophile movement, which provided a framework for LGBT civil rights activism in the United States, can trace its roots back to the 1950s, when the Mattachine Society, the Daughters of Bilitis and ONE Inc. were founded. In 1963, homophile corporations in New York, Philadelphia and Washington, D.C. joined together to form East Coast Homophile Organizations (ECHO), *in an effort to more closely coordinate their activities. The creation of ECHO inspired other homophile organizations in the US to explore the idea of forming a national homophile institution.*

In 1966, the North American Conference of Homophile Organizations (NACHO) was formed. NACHO held annual conferences, helped start dozens of local gay groups across the country and issued position papers on a variety of LGBT-related issues. It organized national demonstrations, including a May 1966 action against military discrimination that included the country's first gay motorcade. NACHO challenged anti-gay laws and regulations ranging from immigration issues and military service to the legality of serving alcohol to homosexuals.

NACHO disbanded after a contentious 1970 convention at which older contributors and younger individuals, proposing more radical actions in the wake of the 1969 Stonewall riots, clashed. Homosexual Sunshine magazine declared the conference "the war that ended the homophile movement." The Stonewall riots, of course, is a term that refers to a response from the gay community to protest New York City police turning to violence when raiding gay and lesbian bars, a common practice in the 1960s.

The founders of these various groups saw themselves as part of a greater liberation movement for all oppressed people. They had no interest in establishing special privileges for gays and lesbians. Nevertheless, they were denied privileges that heterosexuals took for granted. For example, homosexuals were routinely fired from their jobs, evicted from their apartments or homes, jailed on trumped-up charges, harassed by police, and sometimes even beaten in the streets simply because they were gay.

The founders of these organizations felt that gays should organize politically so they could fight back against repression and discrimination. By organizing, they would have more power than individuals acting alone. By acting publicly, they hoped to educate both gay people and heterosexuals about homosexuality. The thought behind forming a national organization was that it would allow them to reach a wider audience. The Stonewall uprising was a tipping point for the gay liberation movement in the United States. In the following days, gay men and lesbians in New York City overlooked gender, race, class, and generational obstacles in an effort to become a cohesive community. Within six months, two gay activist organizations were formed in New York

(Gay Liberation Front and Gay Activists Alliance), plus a homosexual law reform society. Within a year, gay organizations were founded across the US and the world.

Stonewall

In New York, Greenwich Village and Harlem were the hubs of large, lively gay and lesbian groups. Police raids and harassment were common within the city. Liquor licenses for homosexual bars were unfairly eliminated. There were also a variety of initiatives in which undercover officers were deployed, with a goal of entrapping gay men. These initiatives would often result in solicitation charges and/or jail time. Although raids and harassment were not uncommon, gay bars had been one of very few secure refuges for homosexuals to go out, loosen up and feel safe.

When raids took place, the police would often be overly violent. People were frequently pushed roughly up against a wall and asked to supply identification. Anyone who could not present an identification that aligned with current societal perceptions would be charged and arrested. This typically covered drag queens, and trans-women and trans-men.

The Stonewall Riots, also called the Stonewall Uprising, began in the early hours of June 28, 1969, when New York City police raided the Stonewall Inn, a gay club located in Greenwich Village in New York City. The raid sparked a riot among bar patrons and neighborhood residents as police roughly hauled employees and patrons out of the bar. It led to six days of protests and violent clashes with law enforcement outside the bar on Christopher Street, in the neighboring streets and in Christopher Park, which is located nearby. The Stonewall Riots served as a catalyst for the gay rights movement in the US and around the world. The Stonewall riots and protests sparked an international movement for homosexual rights that has only grown since then.

It is also worth pointing out that the first gay pride parades were held to commemorate the first anniversary of the Stonewall Riots. Initially held only in Chicago, Los Angeles, New York and San Francisco, in June of 1970, the celebration of gay pride in late June is now common in cities across the US and around the world. A monument to commemorate the riots was erected at the site in 2016 and the police commissioner for New York City finally issued a public apology for the event in 2019.

roughly up against a wall and asked to supply identification. Anyone who could not present an identification that aligned with current societal perceptions would be charged and arrested. This typically covered drag queens, and trans-women and trans-men.

The Stonewall Riots, also called the Stonewall Uprising, began in the early hours of June 28, 1969, when New York City police raided the Stonewall Inn, a gay club located in Greenwich Village in New York City. The raid sparked a riot among bar patrons and neighborhood residents as police roughly hauled employees and patrons out of the bar. It led to six days of protests and violent clashes with law enforcement outside the bar on Christopher Street, in the neighboring streets and in Christopher Park, which is located nearby. The Stonewall Riots served as a catalyst for the gay rights movement in the US and around the world. The Stonewall riots and protests sparked an international movement for homosexual rights that has only grown since then.

It is also worth pointing out that the first gay pride parades were held to commemorate the first anniversary of the Stonewall Riots. Initially held only in Chicago, Los Angeles, New York and San Francisco, in June of 1970, the celebration of gay pride in late June is now common in cities across the US and around the world. A monument to commemorate the riots was erected at the site in 2016 and the police commissioner for New York City finally issued a public apology for the event in 2019.

The Impact of the Stonewall Rebellion

The Stonewall Riots were a turning point for the gay community. It spurred movements in New York and across the globe. The aftermath brought with it a new sense of activism, in which three newspapers focused on safeguarding the rights of gay men and women were immediately founded. A number of activist groups were launched using openly confrontational tactics that would have been spurned in prior years. Gay rights organizations such as the Mattachine Society and the Daughters of Bilitis had existed since the 1950s, though these organizations had historically used a softer approach.

In the days following Stonewall, gay men and lesbians in New York City gelled into a more cohesive community. Historically, each group had viewed the other as something completely separate. Within six months, two gay activist organizations were formed in New York (Gay Liberation Front and Gay Activists Alliance), plus a homosexual law reform society. Within a year, gay organizations were founded across the US and the world.

Christopher Street Liberation Day Parade, 1970. (Photo: Kay Tobin via NYPL)

The Gay Liberation Front (GLF) and Gay Activists Alliance (GAA) are two organizations that were created in the aftermath of the Stonewall Riots. These two advocacy groups used more forceful strategies than their predecessors. Aside from organizing public protests, members of these groups would debate with politicians and other leaders in public forums. This forced the leadership to acknowledge the problems the gay community was facing and deliver their responses publicly.

The Stonewall Riots gave birth to Pride Month. Christopher Avenue Liberation Day was created on June 28, 1970, to mark the first anniversary of the Stonewall Riots. The march that took place in Chicago, Los Angeles, New York and San Francisco in June of 1970 would become known as the first gay pride parades in support of ending discrimination against the LGBTQ community. In 2019, New York led a worldwide celebration recognizing the 50th anniversary of the Stonewall Riots. It was attended by over five million people in New York alone, marking a positive step toward acceptance and equal rights.

Stonewall Inn National memorial

Activism after the Stonewall Uprising

In the aftermath of the Stonewall Uprising, activists in New York City formed a variety of organizations to push for LGBT rights. Some groups focused on specific issues, such as the Gay Liberation Front (GLF), which sought to promote an anti-establishment lifestyle and ideology. Other groups were more politically oriented or had specific agendas, such as STAR, which stood for Street Transvestite Action Revolutionaries. The Lesbian Feminist Liberation movement was also born during this time.

The Gay Activists Alliance (GAA) was formed soon after the Stonewall Uprising by dissident members of the GLF to focus on militant action, including picketing and demonstrations. In 1970, the group announced plans for a citywide gay strike, in which no gay-owned business would be open on June 28. The groups held several protests against government agencies that did not acknowledge gay employees and organized a march to commemorate the first anniversary of Stonewall. The GAA also campaigned to make homosexuality acceptable in society and worked with other organizations to fight discrimination against gays in employment and housing.

The Gay Rights National Lobby was established in Washington, DC. With a full-time staff and a network of volunteers around the country, it lobbied Congress to pass laws that would fight discrimination based on sexual orientation. Their efforts helped to defeat a constitutional amendment that would have banned gay marriage nationwide by defining marriage as "a union between one man and one woman."

Workplace Culture

There's no question that workplace culture has witnessed substantial change over the last few years as a result of the rising demand for LGBTQIA+ rights. The negative stigma that surrounded this group of people for years has been steadily fading away as more and more people in the workplace come out about their sexual identities and preferences.

The LGBTQIA+ community is made up of more than just gay people. Recent advances in understanding gender, sexual orientation, and identity have led to a growing recognition that a wide range of identities fall outside traditional conceptions of heterosexuality and two-gender associations.

The term LGBT was first used in 1988 by activists seeking to create an inclusive banner under which all would feel welcome. Since then, the term has grown to encompass an even wider spectrum of identities; however, this initial description is still relevant today.

In the early days of the LGBTQ movement, many companies were reluctant to hire openly LGBTQ employees. The environment was not only hostile but also discriminatory. Before the Civil Rights Act of 1964, which made it illegal to discriminate based on race, religion, sex, or national origin, people could be fired simply because of being gay. The example of Stonewall also illustrates that discriminatory practices continued beyond the passing of the Act.

Through the efforts of activists like Barbara Gittings and Frank Kameny in the 1960s, more open-minded employers began to realize that sexual orientation and/or gender identity have nothing to do with a person's ability to perform a job. As a result, these employers started creating internal policies and practices that treated LGBTQ employees fairly and protected them from discrimination.

For years, LGBTQ people have been at the forefront of social and political change in the US. It was not until all that recently, however, that discrimination and harassment against LGBTQ people became less common in the workplace.

As recently as 2014, fewer than half of the states had anti-discrimination laws protecting LGBTQ employees. In a Pew Research Center survey conducted the same year, only about a third of lesbian, gay, and bisexual people reported feeling comfortable in regard to being open about their sexual orientation at work.

The progress made since then has been remarkable. Today, more than two-thirds of survey respondents in the US support laws that would protect LGBTQ people from discrimination in jobs, public accommodations and housing, according to Pew Research Center. It is also telling that currently, 88 percent of American adults say they personally know someone who is lesbian, gay, or bisexual. This number represents a significant increase from the 61 percent that was reported in 1993.

The Supreme Court's 2015 Obergefell v. Hodges decision, which found that same-sex couples have a constitutional right to marry, has also fueled significant changes in attitudes about LGBTQ rights among many Americans, including Republicans. In a report from 2016, it was found that just over half of surveyed Republicans (54 percent) believed that businesses should not be allowed to refuse services to gay or lesbian people.

The New York Times published a piece about the history of LGBTQ issues in the workplace dating back to the 1930s and 1940s. The article details how these groups have historically been forced to conceal their identity, especially at work. This resulted in drinking establishments becoming one of the only places where gay people could feel safe and build community. The article chronicles one of the first gay organizations in the US, the Daughters of Bilitis, which was established in San Francisco in 1955. The group was formed by two women who were denied entry into an exclusively lesbian bar. They created their own group, which was largely focused on socializing and providing community for other lesbian women.

In the modern era, organizations such as Out & Equal and Pride at Work have become well-known advocacy groups in the struggle for LGBTQIA+ rights in the workplace. These groups are important insofar as they have been able to create safe spaces for gay employees to share experiences and figure out how to support each other.

One of the most important battlegrounds in the fight for LGBTQIA+ equality has been the workplace. In the past, sexual orientation and gender identity were not considered protected classes by federal law, and many companies had openly bigoted policies in regards to hiring and firing employees. Being gay, lesbian, or transgender was a justifiable cause for termination and discrimination was pervasive in many businesses.

The fight for equality in the workplace has made tremendous progress in recent decades. But there is still much progress to be made. Some of the most prominent organizations in the modern economy are known for their support of LGBTQIA+ employees. These businesses recognize that making the workplace safe, inclusive and accepting for LGBTQIA+ employees can help to attract top talent and retain the best workers.

Being gay in the workplace is easier now than it was in previous years. Unfortunately, however, it is still common to see headlines about discrimination lawsuits due to sexual orientation. In fact, around 40 percent of Americans maintain the belief that sexual orientation could be a potentially allowable reason for terminating an employee.

Gay rights have come a long way since the time when homosexuality was treated with fear, shame and outright hostility. Even in the modern era, people who identify as lesbian, gay, bisexual, transgender, or asexual (LGBTQIA+) continue to face prejudice and discrimination. If any progress is ever going to be made toward acceptance and equal rights, then learning the correct terminology would be an important first step.

In many cases, people are unaware of the proper terminology for non-straight or non-cisgender. This is partly why it can be difficult for members of these communities to feel safe and accepted in their communities.

Here are some of the key terms to understand:

- Lesbian - Women whose primary romantic and/or sexual attraction is to other women.
- Gay - This describes people who are attracted romantically or sexually to members of the same sex; however, some men who identify as gay may prefer other terms when describing themselves, such as queer or same-gender-loving.

- Bisexual – This refers to individuals who are physically, romantically and/or emotionally attracted to men and women. The attraction does not have to be equally split between genders, and there may be a preference for one gender over others.
- Pansexual – This term describes individuals with the potential for aesthetic attraction, romantic love, or sexual desire toward people of all gender identities and biological sexes. People who identify as pansexual can be romantically and/or sexually attracted to many different types of people, regardless of sex, gender identity, or gender expression. It is sometimes referred to as omnisexuality.
- Transgender (Trans) – This is a person whose internal sense of self does not match their birth sex.
- Asexual – This refers to a person who doesn't experience sexual attraction to other people. Asexuals may still have a romantic attraction to others, but not necessarily. For example, you can be a-romantic and asexual (no romantic or sexual attraction to others), gray-asexual (experience sexual attraction rarely or only under certain circumstances), or demisexual (require strong emotional bonds before experiencing sexual attraction).
- Intersex – This refers to an individual with sexual characteristics that don't fit medical norms for female or male bodies. For example, they could be born with genitals that resemble both female and male genitalia. They could have internal organs that are typically associated with being either female or male.
- Queer – Though originally considered a derogatory term, queer has been reclaimed by many LGBTQIA+ individuals as an umbrella term for all those who don't identify as heterosexual or cisgender. It can also refer to someone whose gender expression falls outside conventional norms associated with masculinity or femininity.

- Genderqueer – This is someone who doesn't identify as either male or female and may identify as a mix of both genders, neither gender, or something that transcends gender.
- Gender nonconforming – This is a person with a gender expression that differs from stereotypical expectations of masculinity or femininity. They may choose not to conform to society's expectations based on their perceived sex (male or female).
- LGBTQIA+ - Lesbian, gay, bisexual, trans, queer, intersex, and asexual, plus the rest of the gender expressions within the community.
- LGBTQIA - Lesbian, gay, bisexual, trans/transgender/two-spirit/third gender/trans woman or man/trans masculine/ trans feminine or non-binary person, plus intersex and asexual person or ally.

Although the LGBTQIA+ (lesbian, gay, bisexual, transgender, queer/questioning, intersex, and asexual) acronym is widely accepted as an umbrella term to describe all individuals who are not cisgender heterosexuals, some people feel the term is too limiting. For example, both the Human Rights Campaign (HRC) and GLAAD accept LGBTQIA+ as a formal definition of this group, but other activists might define it differently. These individuals often add other terms, such as allies, pansexual, polyamorous, or asexual, to include everyone else who identifies as part of this community.

The goal is for everyone to feel represented in the LGBTQIA+ community. As society continues to progress in the efforts toward building a welcoming and inclusive community, the understanding and acceptance of differing gender/sexual identities will continue to expand.

With that in mind, here are two important tips to remember when referring to these groups:

1. Inclusive language is best – It is advisable to refer to various groups by their full name and not shorten them. For example,

when referring to a group that includes everyone from LGBTQIA+ individuals to heterosexuals, use "LGBTQIA+ and allies" instead of just "LGBTQIA+." Using inclusive language ensures that a particular group does not perceive any bias.

2. Avoid making assumptions – It is unwise to make assumptions in any context. In regard to an individual's sexual orientation and/or gender identity, making assumptions can be especially hurtful. As the saying goes, appearances can be deceiving. Also, there are many people who do not conform to traditional gender roles or stereotypes, and these individuals may look just like anyone else.

When it comes to language, representation is vital. Words matter and the accurate use of terminology can sometimes feel even more important with the LGBTQIA+ community, considering the long history of discrimination this group has faced. Using appropriate terminology and nomenclature makes it possible to recognize, accept and honor the uniqueness of individual community members in our workplace, on our websites and social media platforms.

The world is full of people with differing backgrounds, beliefs and experiences. While individual experiences may not always be relatable, it's important to respect the beliefs and viewpoints of other people, so we can learn about each other and move society toward acceptance.

There are many ways that we can work together to build a more inclusive culture. Using the correct terminology and naming structures associated with sexual orientation and gender identity would be a giant, positive step toward ensuring that all people feel respected, recognized, and included.

Margo Rila and Maggie Rubenstein

Margo Rila and Maggie Rubenstein are two people who significantly advanced the move toward acceptance of the LGBTQ community, especially for bisexuals. Rila was a bisexual activist, an advocate for sexual freedom and a sex counselor. Together with her partner, Frank Rila, she founded the San Francisco Sexual Freedom League in 1967. Margo Rila was also one of the founders of the San Francisco Bisexual Center and San Francisco Sex Information.

Maggie Rubenstein, also a bisexual activist, helped to establish a number of education-based sex institutions. These included Glide Memorial Church's National Sex Forum, the San Francisco Sex Information Hotline, and the Institute for the Advanced Study of Human Sexuality.

Rila and Rubenstein were early pioneers who inspired many others to take up the reins and shed light on the issues and obstacles this community has faced over the years. Their work led the way forward by illuminating the experiences and complexities of this sexual identity for the rest of the world.

The world is full of challenges for the LGBTQIA+ community. Fortunately, however, there are numerous individuals speaking publicly about their experiences in an effort to enhance the mental well-being of their fellow community members. These individuals share their opinions on political issues that impact the LGBTQIA+ community, relating them to anyone who may be dealing with panic, anxiety, or depression. The following individuals have worked to help people unlearn harmful stereotypes and inform on where biases have been historically problematic.

Here are three modern leaders in the LGBTQIA+ community:

Sabine Maxine Lopez

Sabine Maxine Lopez is a Black, non-binary femme who established A Tribe Called Queer, which is a clothing brand that sells items with messages promoting immigrant rights and gender equality.

Based in Los Angeles, Lopez hopes to create a space for marginalized groups who may not feel represented by the media. Lopez wants to inspire people to feel encouraged and supported in the journey to find their personal truth, especially in conservative communities.

Tyler Oakley

Tyler Oakley has earned renown for his short videos on YouTube. There, he advocates for LGBTQIA+ issues and raises awareness about items of concern to the LGBTQIA+ community. Oakley is a well-known activist, a philanthropist and fundraiser for multiple organizations.

His success has translated into a career in radio and television, which he uses as a platform to raise awareness about LGBTQIA+ issues. Oakley famously raised over $1 million in funds for the Trevor Project, which provides crisis intervention and suicide prevention services to LGBTQIA+ youth. In 2014, he was named one of Time magazine's "100 Most Influential People on the Internet."

Tyler Oakley has had a profound impact on the lives of many young people who identify as LGBTQIA+. He provides an honest, entertaining and hopeful look into the lives of queer people that is often missing from mainstream media.

Kenny Ethan Jones

Kenny Ethan Jones is a model, activist, and entrepreneur who says he owes his career in activism to being the first openly transgender man on a period-themed advertisement. The visibility led Jones to be the first trans-individual and the first openly transgender man to speak about menstruation in interviews. His advocacy has been instrumental in normalizing menstrual care for people with mental health conditions and helping menstruation feel like a natural part of life for cisgender menstruators (people who are assigned female at birth), as well as transgender men.

When Instagram decided to implement policies on deadnaming and misgendering, the company reached out to Jones for input, as he is a key figure in the LGBTQIA+ community. Though neither term is recognized in Microsoft Word, both are in the Merriam-Webster dictionary. In the text, deadnaming is defined as referring to a transgender person with the name they were given at birth and haven't used since transitioning. Misgendering refers to the act of using the wrong pronouns when referring to a transsexual or transgender person. Jones was asked to discuss his experiences navigating these issues on Instagram and suggest ways the platform could provide better protections for people like him.

Along with their peers, these leaders have made numerous positive strides in the effort to raise awareness and advocate for equality for the LGBTQIA+ community in all spheres of life. Unfortunately, however, discrimination against this community is still pervasive, even in the workplace.

Anonymous Harassment and Discriminatory experiences

"I was...working for a small-town local insurance organization. A woman I worked with and I were having a casual communication and she made a discriminatory statement about homosexuals. I informed her that I was bisexual and she cut the conversation off immediately. In a matter of days, the owner fired me."

-White cisgender bisexual woman from Kentucky

"Due to the fact I'm gay and trans I got fired and was blackmailed to depart."

-Black transgender homosexual man from New Jersey

"My boss was clearly interested in dating me and...I used to be lesbian. Once I ultimately told him [that], he fired me."

-Latinx cisgender lesbian from Connecticut

"I was let go from a private golf establishment. The sentiment was that my being gay interfered with my capabilities as a bartender."

-White cisgender lesbian from Illinois

"I used to be harassed and when I ultimately complained, I was fired."

-Latinx cisgender bisexual man from Utah

"[I was] fired from my favorite process because my boss disagreed with my sexual orientation."

-Black cisgender gay man from Alabama

[It] became the worst task in my existence. Not only did I lose the task I loved, I lost all the friends and long-lasting relationships I had created with this activity."

-White cisgender bisexual woman from Maine

Apart from being terminated or passed over for employment, respondents mentioned many other forms of unfair treatment. This unfair treatment was primarily based on sexual orientation and gender identity. Discriminatory actions varied from not receiving promotions or pay increases, receiving unequal treatment compared to distinct-intercourse companions, and being excluded from corporate events.

The numbers show that a variety of changes need to occur before the members of the LGBTQIA+ community are treated equally in the workplace and the broader society. A recent survey found that nearly half of all LGBTQIA+ employees had experienced discrimination at work because of their sexuality. The number of transgender people that reported facing discriminatory practices was nearly 60 percent.

Verbal abuse was the most common form of unfair treatment/ discrimination. A number of survey respondents also felt they had been treated unfairly, compared to their heterosexual colleagues.

Nearly 20 percent of survey respondents indicated they knew someone who had been dismissed from their job because of sexual orientation or gender identity. Others said they had been harassed by both colleagues and customers.

To fight these issues and encourage others to come out at work, some companies have created policies that ban discrimination against LGBTQIA+ employees. Unfortunately, however, this does not mean that all companies with such policies are safe environments for those who identify as LGBTQIA+.

In a recent survey, approximately 80 percent of people worldwide said they are heterosexual. In a number of studies, around one to two percent reported that they were not cisgender, meaning their gender identity did not match their sex at birth. This makes it not all that surprising to learn that the broader global society is heteronormative, meaning that heterosexuality is viewed as the normal sexuality. In the Merriam-Webster dictionary, normal is defined as conforming to a standard, usual, typical or expected. Within the discipline of statistics, for something to qualify as normal, it has to come in around 95 percent. A discussion of what is normal is beyond the scope of this book. Regardless of semantics or what the broader society considers to be typical or expected, it is very uncommon for enlightened individuals to embrace a viewpoint or behavior that could be considered discriminatory or unfair. Though it is unfair to generalize, it is not exactly a groundbreaking idea to state the people often fear what they do not understand, and this often leads to discrimination and unfair treatment. A valid justification for this type of behavior does not exist, and it is unfortunate that LGBTQIA+ individuals face discrimination and harassment for being different than the heteronormative standard.

A study recently published by the McKinsey Institute showed that transgender people make 32 percent less per year than their cisgender counterparts. It is easy to see why a non-cisgender person would be reluctant to give 100 percent to an organization in the face of this knowledge. To create buy-in from employees and leverage the benefits of diversity, it is important to ensure that the workplace is a safe space for members of the LGBTQIA+ community. Company leadership should focus on eliminating harassment and discrimination as it is negatively impactful to job performance, along with the fact that doing so is simply the right thing to do. A fear of discrimination and unfair treatment can prevent individuals from coming out at work or asking their colleagues to use the appropriate pronouns when referring to them.

Unfair treatment and discrimination can lead to stress and anxiety—even suicidal thoughts. After all, people spend the vast majority of their time in the workplace. If the environment for people at work is negative, it is highly likely this negativity will spread into other aspects of their lives.

Many businesses and institutions already have antidiscrimination policies in place. There are also Federal laws in place to protect members of the LGBTQIA+ community from discrimination. Unfortunately, however, nearly 75 percent of LGBTQIA+ workers report hearing jokes about lesbian or gay people at work and around 50 percent report that they have been harassed. It may be impossible to legislate ethics or morality, but clearly, something needs to be done to change the pervasive attitudes that result in discrimination and unfair treatment.

The LGBTQIA+ community has been fighting for equality in the workplace for years. Many positive strides have been made in the movement toward acceptance and equality. Unfortunately, however, it is still not uncommon for members of the LGBTQIA+ community to face discrimination, harassment and other forms of bias.

Impacts In Higher Education and The Workplace

In a landmark case from 2020, the Supreme Court ruled that the Civil Rights Act of 1964 protects homosexuals and transgender people from workplace discrimination. Since its passing, the Civil Rights Act had protected people from discrimination based on race, color, religion, sex or national origin. The update from 2020 by the Court made it clear that employment discrimination based on LGBTQIA+ identification is illegal. Prior to the decision, 21 states had laws banning discrimination based on sexual orientation and gender identity. Around half of the LGBTQIA+ population lived in states where they were not protected from discrimination before the ruling.

These laws affect people of all ages. Harassment and discrimination on university campuses is pervasive. The effects are so extensive that it makes it necessary for people to have access to financial resources, counseling, mental fitness offerings, and public advantages in order to achieve educational success. In a survey from 2019, around 65 percent of transgender, nonbinary/genderqueer, undecided, or unlisted undergraduate students reported experiencing harassing behavior upon enrollment.

Individuals in the LGBTQIA+ community routinely face discrimination in society and especially in the workplace. Systemic racism and stereotypical ideologies about minority groups continue to plague our workplaces and the LGBTQIA+ community is no different. To increase diversity and organizational effectiveness, leaders should work to ensure that minority groups and those with lower incomes have access to a quality postsecondary education.

The Williams Institute at UCLA estimates that of the 13 million people in the United States who identify as a part of LGBTQIA+ community, 5.6 percent identified as American Indian and/or Alaskan Native, 4.6 percent as Black, 6 percent as Latinx, and 4.4 percent as Asian/Pacific Islander. There are an estimated 8.1 million LGBTQIA+ employees in the Unites States.

Great strides have been made in the advancement of civil rights. Still, members of the LGBTQIA+ community, people of color and many others continue to endure racial inequalities, even though there are already many laws in place that were designed to ensure equal rights. That is why it's imperative for Federal, state, and local policy makers to continue to fight for legal guidelines, regulations, and practices that protect and support minority groups, including equity and equality in the workplace.

9

Workplace LGBTQIA+ Discrimination and Harassment

Discrimination is hate, and there is no place for it in the workplace. Strive to be a person or organization who promotes diversity and commits to sustaining an inclusive culture.

—Germany Kent

A workplace free of harassment and discrimination is a right that every employee deserves. Most discriminatory practices are based on prejudices and stereotypes about groups of people. The result is that minorities are typically the most at risk for experiencing discrimination in the workplace.

In the United States, it is illegal to discriminate based on age, race, ethnicity, national origin, sex, disability, or religion. Unfortunately, it is not uncommon for the average American worker to face discrimination in the workplace, despite legal protection under a series of antidiscrimination laws.

The US Equal Employment Opportunity Commission (EEOC) is the Federal agency that enforces discrimination laws in the workplace. The EEOC enforces laws that make it illegal to discriminate against an employee or job applicant because of race, color, religion, sex (including pregnancy), national origin, age (forty or older), disability, or genetic information. The EEOC also enforces Federal laws that make it illegal to retaliate against an employee for filing a charge of discrimination, participating in a discrimination investigation or lawsuit, or otherwise opposing employment discrimination.

The EEOC is the first stop for individuals who believe they have been discriminated against in the workplace. People who believe they were discriminated against and want to file a lawsuit in court must start by filing a charge with the EEOC. It is also a requirement that claimants have to give the agency enough time to investigate the claim.

Employers should take the necessary steps to prevent and correct discriminatory and/or harassing conduct. Examples of preventive measures could potentially include:

- Creating an explicit policy that shows the employer prohibits discrimination and harassment based on sexual orientation, gender identity or gender expression. A complaint process for employees to follow should also be established.
- Clearly communicating to employees their expectations for policy compliance.
- Making it clear to employees that any violation of the policy will not be tolerated. A disciplinary process should be established.

- A statement in the EEO policy prohibiting discrimination based on gender identity, gender expression and/or sexual orientation.
- Training managers about the particulars of the employer's EEO policies, including those pertaining to harassment based on sexual orientation, gender identity, or gender expression.

Another proactive means of reducing the prevalence of discrimination and harassment would be to assemble an employee resource group. This strategy could involve having a group of key employees educate their colleagues about issues related to sexual orientation and/or gender identity.

An employer should take immediate investigatory action if an instance of misconduct or harassment occurs. The scope of the investigation, of course, would depend on the allegations. In some cases, an employer may only need to interview the complainant and respondent. In others, it may be necessary to interview outside witnesses or examine relevant documents. An employer should notify the complainant and respondent about the general subject matter of the allegations so that each party can prepare an adequate response. It is unnecessary to provide all of the details to each of the involved parties, however. Investigating offenses is important, but so is protecting employee privacy. Privacy regulations are in place to ensure that employers only disclose information to those with a need to know.

The LGBTQIA+ community is one of the most underrepresented groups in the workplace. Legal protections for this group are already in place; however, discrimination is still rampant, especially in the United States. Employers should work to create a workplace environment that is safe and inclusive for everyone.

Workplace discrimination is any act that violates equal employment opportunity laws. These laws were created to prevent employers from unjustly discriminating against employees based on certain characteristics. While most antidiscrimination laws only apply to employers with at least fifteen employees, some also apply to smaller companies. For example, sexual harassment claims can be brought against employers with less than fifteen employees.

It's important for workers to know their rights when it comes to discrimination in the workplace. The following is an overview of major Federal antidiscrimination laws and how these laws were designed to protect workers from unfair treatment on the job.

Employees are protected from discrimination by the Civil Rights Act of 1964. The act prohibits discrimination based on race, color, religion, sex, or national origin. It also prohibits retaliation for filing a discrimination complaint or for participating in an investigation related to a complaint.

The Equal Pay Act of 1963 (EPA), as amended, protects men and women who perform substantially equal work in the same establishment from sex-based wage differentials. Under the EPA, employers may not pay unequal wages to men and women who perform jobs that require substantially equal skill, effort, and responsibility under similar working conditions within the same establishment.

The Pregnancy Discrimination Act of 1978 prohibits employers from discriminating against workers because they are pregnant or have recently given birth. Employers must provide accommodations such as more frequent breaks and more time off to pregnant workers if they provide similar accommodations to other workers who need it due to medical conditions.

The Age Discrimination in Employment Act of 1967 protects employees age 40 and older from being discriminated against based on their age. It also prohibits retaliation against an employee who files a complaint regarding age discrimination.

Title VII of the Civil Rights Act of 1964 prohibits employers from discriminating based on religion, race, color, or national origin. Title VII also prohibits retaliation for filing a complaint about religious discrimination or participating in an investigation related to religious discrimination.

Title I and Title V of the Americans with Disabilities Act

of 1990 prohibit employment discrimination against qualified individuals with disabilities in the private sector and in state and local governments.

The difference between harassment and discrimination is often confused. Although there are a number of similarities between the terms, there are some key differences. Harassment is illegal and a violation of Federal law. Discrimination, on the other hand, is not a criminal offense, though it is also illegal. The terms have different meanings, even though they are often used interchangeably. It is important to understand the differences because the law treats harassment and discrimination differently.

Discrimination occurs when an individual is treated less favorably than another person in a similar situation because of a protected attribute, such as race, sex, or disability. Discrimination can be a standalone practice and/or occurrence, or it can result from the application of neutral rules and policies that adversely affect people with a particular attribute.

While discrimination could refer to something an individual may not be aware of at the time, harassment is typically apparent. The term harassment refers to a type of employment discrimination that involves unwanted or inappropriate behavior in the workplace. The behavior can be directed at an employee based on race, gender, disability, or any other protected class.

Unwelcome conduct may include offensive remarks about a person's protected status. The law does not prohibit simple teasing, offhand comments or isolated incidents that are not very serious in nature. Once a behavior becomes so frequent and/or severe that it creates a hostile/offensive work environment, or results in an adverse employment decision, that is when the harassment becomes illegal. The following describes the different forms that harassment and discrimination can take.

Discrimination

The term discrimination means to distinguish, single out, or make a distinction between persons or things on the basis of a class or category. It occurs when implicit biases, prejudices (personal and institutional), and stereotypes lead to various forms of unfair treatment. This could be unequal treatment in regards to hiring practices, promotions, job assignments, terminations or compensation. Discrimination could also refer to the allocation of resources, denial of access to said resources, social exclusion, and various forms of harassment.

In the context of employment, the law defines discrimination as any unfavorable treatment based on several characteristics, including, but not limited to, sex, age, race, color, national origin, religion, disability, or pregnancy. Discrimination can take many forms—it doesn't have to be blatant or intentional. In fact, it may be more subtle and go unnoticed by others. It can be as obvious as someone saying something inappropriate or racist in the workplace. But it could also be as simple as an employer only inviting younger employees to social gatherings after work (age discrimination).

There are two main types of employment discrimination: disparate treatment and disparate impact. Disparate treatment involves a policy or practice that treats some people less favorably than others because of a protected characteristic. An example would be if an employer gave all female employees lower performance reviews than male employees simply because of their gender.

Disparate impact occurs when an employer's policy or practice appears to be neutral, but there is no legitimate business reason for the policy or practice, and it results in an adverse impact on members of a protected class. For example, if a company only hires people who speak English fluently, and this requirement has a negative impact on people of a particular nationality, it may be discriminatory unless speaking English in the workplace is necessary for business purposes.

Harassment

When it comes to harassment, the line between what is viewed as acceptable behavior and what is viewed as unacceptable behavior can sometimes be difficult to determine. It is not uncommon to see discriminatory practices and sexual harassment depicted in TV shows and the movie industry. The media shapes societal beliefs about how these actions should be handled, in addition to how people should respond to them. What many don't realize, however, is that harassment does not refer to only two forms of discrimination. Harassment is not limited to just one type of behavior; in fact, it has many manifestations.

The following are typical examples of workplace harassment:

- Verbal harassment – The most common form of harassment, this includes derogatory comments or insults about a person's race, ethnicity, sex, age, disability, or any other characteristic.
- Physical harassment – This only makes up a small percentage of reported cases, although physical violence can include more than just assault; it may include unwanted touching or more subtle acts, basically anything that elicits a fear response.
- Quid pro quo harassment – This refers to a 'this for that' exchange, such as when a benefit or reward is conditioned on an employee submitting to unwelcome sexual advances. For example, if an employee were denied a promotion unless she went on a date with her boss, that would be quid pro quo harassment.
- Visual harassment – Any image that could be deemed harassing in nature could be considered workplace harassment. Examples include lewd pictures, racially offensive symbols, etc.
- Sexual harassment – This could include unwanted sexual advances, sexual jokes or remarks, and other sexually oriented behavior that creates a hostile work environment.

- **Gender-based harassment** – Though this is more frequently aimed at women, it could include any form of behavior that is negatively impactful toward men or women, such as verbally abusing an individual for non-conformance to stereotypical male or female roles in the workplace.
- **Racial and ethnic harassment** – Examples of this include offensive comments about minorities or cultural differences, racial or ethnic slurs, or jokes about someone's accent.
- **Religious harassment** – This involves any form of behavior that is centered on an individual's religious beliefs and/or practices.
- **Disability-related harassment** – This refers to verbal or physical abuse that is based on an individual's mental or physical disability.
- **Microaggressions and microassaults** – This refers to a form of negative behavior designed to seem innocuous at first. Though this form of harassment may initially escape the attention of the targeted individual, after a moment of reflection, the intended negative impact of the comment or action becomes clear.
- **Retaliation harassment** – This refers to any action that has a negative impact on an employee who has reported experiencing harassment. Retaliation is taken very seriously in statutory and common law jurisdictions since it potentially undermines the core purpose of antidiscrimination statutes, which are designed to prevent future discrimination. Employees dealing with retaliation should be sure to make reports early, accurately, and whenever possible, in writing. Individuals facing retaliation from a hostile work environment or reporting entity should contact the EEOC and/or an attorney. Employers dealing with employees with ongoing performance issues should document all instances of negative performance if the goal is termination, as this could help to avoid a retaliation claim.

The costs associated with workplace discrimination and harassment can quickly spiral. Some of the costs are easy to measure and others have a more intrinsic impact, making them more difficult to quantify. The costs related to lost productivity, legal fees and medical expenses are relatively easy to determine. Conversely, other costs such as low employee morale, customer dissatisfaction and loss of reputation are more difficult to measure. The following is a list of negative outcomes that result from workplace discrimination and/ or harassment:

- **Productivity losses** – This can result from a variety of factors, such as a lack of belief in company leadership and/or an instance of violence in the workplace, basically anything that distracts or impedes an employee's ability to focus on the task at hand.
- **Employee turnover** – A reported instance of discrimination or harassment will have a negative impact on a company's reputation, whether the claim is valid or invalid, though a valid claim will obviously have more of an impact. Potential staff members will consider other opportunities and current employees will look for the exit, dramatically increasing the costs associated with recruitment/retention.
- **Employee absenteeism** – Absences, tardiness, vacation time and sick time can all result when an employee feels that they are the victim of harassment and/or discrimination. Further, an employee who reports a claim, whether valid or not, could potentially influence their colleagues to adopt similar behavior.
- **Decreased employee morale** – A staff member alleging or experiencing discrimination and/or harassment is unlikely to have positive morale. Even the knowledge a claim exists can have a detrimental impact on overall employee morale, making it less likely the staff will buy into the organizational mission. This can obviously make recruitment/retention initiatives more difficult. Employers interested in preventing

negative outcomes should make it clear that harassment and discrimination will not be tolerated and communicate their efforts toward alleviating these problems to the staff.

- Litigation risks – Employers that allow workplace harassment to occur, use discriminatory practices or fire whistleblowers open the door to a variety of legal expenses. Even if a claim is ultimately proved to be invalid, the costs associated with fighting it can be substantial.

The following list describes behaviors that could be construed as harassment:

- **Offensive jokes**
- **Racial/ethnic slurs**
- **Intimidation or threats**
- **Ridicule/mockery**
- **Derogatory comments**
- **Offensive objects/pictures**
- **Interference with work performance**
- **Offensive gestures**

Actions to take against workplace harassment:

1. **Both employers and employees should keep a detailed account of the events that transpired, including names and dates.**
2. **Employees should provide their supervisor or another company leader with information about the behavior, preferably in writing.**
3. **All of the details associated with the event should be documented in writing by the employee and the employer.**
4. **If possible, find a witness.**
5. **Employees should follow up with their supervisor or another company leader to ensure appropriate action was taken, in writing.**

6. File a complaint with the Equal Employment Opportunity Commission (EEOC).

7. In many cases, the EEOC will assign an attorney to pursue a claim if it is believed to be valid. If not, it could be worthwhile to contact an attorney in regard to filing a private lawsuit.

Note: Steps six and seven should only be taken if the appropriate action is not taken by the employer.

While it may be impossible to know exactly how many people are being abused in the workplace, there is no shortage of resources available to assist those who need help dealing with harassment.

There are a number of company policies and procedures that could be adopted to help protect employees from harassment. Ensuring that the company hiring process is non-discriminatory is a good first step. It is also advisable to set clear expectations, include language in the employee handbook that harassment/ discrimination will not be tolerated, and offer professional training exercises for all employees. Doing so can help to prevent workplace issues from occurring, send a message to the staff that these actions are unacceptable, and provide them with an idea of how to respond to a variety of possible scenarios.

Ultimately, the goal is to create a culture of respect in which all of the participants know that harassment and discrimination will not be tolerated. Further, this can help to ensure that everyone on the team, from company leadership and middle management to entry-level employees and interns, has a shared understanding of what kinds of behavior are acceptable and appropriate at work.

10

Unconscious Bias

I think unconscious bias is one of the
hardest things to get at.
—Ruth Bader Ginsburg

Bias can be defined as the general tendency to act or think in a predictable manner. Everyone in the world has a different viewpoint, and the brain has a tendency to sort information based on preconceived ideas. This is due to the fact that doing so vastly simplifies the cognitive process.

As a result, everyone sees the world through a different lens. Whether this lens is conscious or subconscious, the result is that individuals and groups often judge the same information in different ways, as opinions and beliefs are shaped by previously held values and assumptions. For example, if an individual believes that some groups are lazy or untrustworthy, it is more likely that ambiguous behavior will be interpreted as a sign of laziness or untrustworthiness.

Bias does not always occur at a conscious level. In fact, it typically occurs at an unconscious or implicit level. A person may hold negative stereotypes about a group of people under the surface, yet on a conscious level think all people are equal. Implicit bias can be detected through cognitive tests or by observing the behavior of the individual.

The term unconscious bias gets thrown around a lot, but what does it really mean? And how is it possible to know if a company suffers from it?

Unconscious bias is an implicit attitude or stereotype that an individual may hold about a certain group of people, which impacts behaviors, beliefs and decision-making. Biases may be either positive or negative. Oftentimes, a bias may be activated involuntarily, without an individual's awareness or intentional control. All people hold unconscious beliefs and various social stereotypes about other groups. Many of these biases stem from the brain's tendency to arrange social worlds through categorizing, as previously mentioned.

Simply put, it is just how people are wired. The brain is constantly inundated with sensory information. For the sake of simplicity, the brain has learned to form quick assessments of people and situations based on narrow slices of information.

It's important to recognize that everyone has biases. Whether conscious or unconscious, biases can originate from an individual's cultural background, environment, heritage, peer group and/or experiences. Biases are not confined to just race and ethnicity. Instead, biases can apply to perceptions and opinions about age, gender, nationality, religion, and other topics—even the clothing an individual may be wearing, down to its color and whether it is wrinkled or pressed.

If the goal is to move society toward acceptance and positivity, a critical first step is to recognize that everyone has biases. Being aware that biases have a significant effect on decision making can help an individual move past these previously held beliefs and stereotypes. Understanding that biases operate under the surface, it is worth pointing out that many individuals are blind to their personal biases and/or assumptions.

In a nutshell, unconscious bias is a phenomenon in which the brain automatically assigns value to people or things based on preexisting internalized stereotypes. These biases are ingrained in the brain through experiences and cultural conditioning.

In the workplace, unconscious biases tend to impact hiring practices and decisions regarding promotions. Unconscious biases have a wide array of ripple effects. One unfortunate outcome is that biases have resulted in the underrepresentation of minorities in leadership positions. Another example would be the pay inequity between men and women. An unconscious belief that women are less committed than men due to family obligations would potentially result in lower pay and/or less potential for promotion. Similarly, it is not uncommon for people to assume that certain other groups and/or people are "naturally" better at certain types of tasks because of race, gender, national origin, etc. It is worth pointing out that, in some cases, the stereotype can be positive; consider that women are typically thought of as more compassionate and nurturing than men.

Regardless, stereotyping is usually negatively impactful to the workplace. Some individuals may be overlooked for leadership roles because of a view, whether valid or invalid, that they are too quiet and/or reserved. In the past, it was not uncommon for women and people with certain disabilities to be stereotyped as emotionally unstable. This is continuing to occur and, along with many other preconceived ideas, it has an obvious, negative impact on employment decisions. Recognizing the beliefs that form these biases is the first step toward eliminating them and making progress on the goal of making more objective decisions. By eliminating unconscious biases, it makes it easier to build a diverse team and create a positive culture that attracts top talent.

To understand how to identify unconscious biases, it's helpful to learn more about the various ways these biases are typically categorized:

- Confirmation bias – This occurs when an individual actively looks for information that confirms a previously held belief instead of accepting new information that might be in contradiction. For example, an interviewer may be more likely to hire someone with the same alma mater because of an unconscious belief they have something in common.

- **Affect heuristic** – This is a mental shortcut that results in people making decisions based on feelings and emotions instead of factual information. For example, if a company leader feels negative about an individual for no specific reason other than an emotion or a subconscious belief, it could result in an adverse employment decision.

- **Group attribution error** – This form of bias is the result of a preconceived idea that all the members of a certain group are similar because of their membership in that group; individual differences are ignored.

- **Affinity bias** – This occurs when an individual shows favoritism towards an individual or group that is similar. It can lead to inclusion and diversity initiatives. Negative outcomes can result from affinity bias as it can lead to tokenism and/or exclusion of individuals who are different.

- **Halo effect** – This refers to when a positive trait such as intelligence or attractiveness causes an individual to make assumptions about a person's character. The converse can also apply when a singular negative aspect of a person causes an individual to make broad assumptions about a person.

- **Horn effect** – This is a tendency to assume that one negative trait is an indicator that many other negative traits are present. For example, if a candidate is dressed unprofessionally, the interviewer may assume he or she is incompetent.

- **Stereotyping** – This refers to generalizations that people make about other individuals and groups, based on race, gender, nationality, ethnicity, sexual orientation, or other factors. It is the most common form of unconscious bias in the workplace.

- Conformity bias – This is a tendency to follow the opinions, beliefs and behaviors of the crowd, for fear of social rejection.
- Name bias – This term refers to a tendency among certain groups and individuals to discriminate against others because their first name or surname is associated with a certain race and/or ethnicity. An example would be if a candidate with a more "American" sounding name were picked over a candidate with a more "foreign" sounding name, all else being equal.

Unconscious biases influence everything from hiring decisions to performance reviews and promotions. In fact, some studies suggest that a person's race has more of an influence on their performance evaluations than their ability to do the job.

Understanding the Science behind Unconscious Bias

The knowledge base pertaining to unconscious bias has evolved over time. Recent research has led to a better understanding of the nature of unconscious bias and the tools that are necessary to measure it.

People are wired to form ideas about different people, experiences and situations. Making generalizations simplifies the cognitive process, making it easier to learn new ideas and respond to different situations. Unfortunately, the brain's tendency to categorize and make prejudgments can also result in misguided assumptions and beliefs. For example, if an individual has been assaulted by a member of a certain group, the wronged party may end up believing that all the members of that group are nefarious.

But why does this happen? Why do some people believe one thing is true while others believe something completely different? And why do some people insist their way is right and others are wrong? This is where unconscious bias comes in. Unconscious bias is a scientifically proven, adaptive mechanism that is present in everyone.

The brain uses mental shortcuts to help make decisions quickly and navigate a world that is constantly in flux. The shortcuts used by the brain are called heuristics. Mental shortcuts have an obvious benefit, especially in dangerous situations when there is very little time to react. Driving in traffic and having to respond to someone braking unexpectedly is an example of the benefit of heuristics. The downside is that mental shortcuts can lead to unconscious biases.

Mental shortcuts make it easier to categorize information and make associations between different concepts. In the case of navigating a congested roadway, an unconscious bias can be positive if it helps to avoid a collision. However, in other cases, harboring an unconscious bias can result in an inaccurate or unfair grouping of information, resulting in other negative outcomes such as discrimination.

The idea that people maintain implicit biases is not a new concept. In the 1930s, the psychologist John Ridley Stroop conducted a study in which he asked his subjects to first read names of different colors that were printed in black ink. The second step involved having the subjects read the names of colors, written in a different color ink than what was named, i.e. the term purple might have been printed in red ink. Thirdly, subjects were asked to speak the name of a printed color block. Stroop found that, in the second case where the subjects had to read a color name that conflicted with the ink in which it was printed, there was a significant delay. This has become known as the Stroop effect and it points to the fact that the mind automatically categorizes information, which could serve as a partial explanation for the existence of unconscious biases.

As previously stated, unconscious biases can result in adverse employment decisions. Hiring managers are often tasked with reviewing the qualifications of large pools of candidates. In a case where two candidates with similar qualifications are being compared to each other, unconscious bias could result in the hiring manager picking one over the other, whether that individual is consciously aware of the reason why, or not.

The Horn and Halo Effects

The horn and halo effects are cognitive errors that influence the perceptions that people maintain about other individuals and/ or groups. The result of the horn and halo effects are that people sometimes end up viewing all the members of a certain group through a positive or negative lens, instead of a complex mix of both positive and negative characteristics. Essentially, this means that if an individual has a good feeling regarding another individual, the likelihood of ascribing positive traits to that person increases. Likewise, if an individual has a bad feeling regarding another individual, the likelihood of ascribing negative traits to that person increases.

The halo effect was made famous by the psychologist Edward Thorndike in 1920. It has generally been studied in terms of physical attractiveness; those with higher levels of attractiveness have usually been thought of as having positive qualities in other areas. Similarly, survey respondents have felt that those with lower levels of attractiveness have less favorable qualities in other areas.

In his research, Thorndike asked a number of commanding officers to rate their soldiers on a variety of factors, including their physical fitness, hygiene, energy, intellect, capacity for leadership, responsibility, loyalty, and more. Soldiers with higher levels of physical fitness consistently received higher marks in the areas of intelligence, character and leadership.

Viewed through a modern lens, it seems obvious that physical beauty and/or fitness does not equate to other positive attributes. Of course, this is at least partially due to Thorndike's research. It points to the fact that unconscious biases, by definition, are not apparent. This makes it difficult to avoid letting unconscious biases impact beliefs and decision-making.

In recent years, the halo effect has been studied in more detail. Many have expanded its reach to include businesses, countries, brands and products. The halo effect associated with Apple products is a famous example. The halo effect has also been studied in terms of how any positive characteristic can cause it, such as likability or trustworthiness.

It seems appropriate that the halo effect has occasionally been referred to as the halo error. It is easy to see how it could have a negative impact on purchasing decisions as well as many different kinds of relationships, including romantic partners, managers and employees, teachers and students, parents and children.

Biases can be damaging to relationships because of the potential it creates to overlook positive qualities in favor of negative attributes. Reversing unconscious biases is difficult as many individuals are not aware of the biases that drive their decision-making. Also, many individuals who make the halo error in terms of their perception about an individual, business entity or corporation may be willing to look past negative behavior or seek to explain it away, as the effect is pervasive and it is difficult for many to break away from initial perceptions.

Impact of Horn and Halo Effects when Interviewing Candidates

Hiring is a nasty, error-prone process. It is difficult to evaluate one person's qualifications and compare those qualifications to other candidates. Performing this task in aggregate is even harder.

While most interviewers would like to think they are objective, research shows that they are not. Interviewers are influenced by the horn effect as well as the halo effect. When it comes to interviewing job candidates, biases can be negatively impactful. Interviewers are constantly subjected to the horn effect and halo effect when starting their interviews.

A candidate may have an array of positive qualifications, but if that individual arrives late or has a disheveled appearance, it may be difficult for the interviewer to form an accurate assessment. If the interviewer forms a negative opinion from the outset, then that opinion will likely have an influence on every aspect of the interview.

This is the horn effect and, to understand why it is harmful, one need only look to the example of Albert Einstein, who always had wild hair and famously wore the same clothes every day later in life.

An interviewer judging Einstein on his appearance might have been reluctant about hiring him. Being the one who passed over an individual like Einstein is the stuff of nightmares for HR professionals. The example points to the importance of first impressions and how these impressions can be misleading. It is worth pointing out that the halo effect has the potential to be equally damaging, as physical attractiveness and/or a neat appearance does not equate to a positive character.

The Impact of the Horn and Halo Effects on Performance Reviews

Performance reviews can be an important part of the growth process for employees. However, performance reviews can be subject to blind spots and the flawed perceptions of the reviewer. The horn effect can result in the individual doing the performance review giving ratings based on one perceived negative attribute, which unfairly skews the overall results. The halo effect could potentially elevate a mediocre employee to a higher status; the horn effect could limit an employee's growth opportunities.

How to Test for Unconscious Bias

Unconscious bias is pervasive and, as the name implies, present under the surface of an individual's conscious perceptions. This obviously makes it difficult to identify unconscious bias and measure the types of it that may or may not be present in the workplace. There are several ways to measure unconscious bias.

One method that scientists have used to test for the presence of unconscious bias is the Implicit Association Test (IAT). Using a computer, the test measures the time it takes for a person to sort different concepts into two categories, with a goal of figuring out whether unconscious attitudes and hidden preferences are present.

The idea is that people have a "gut feeling" about certain things and will associate them more quickly than others.

The first IAT study was published in 1998. It found that 70 percent of White Americans exhibited an implicit preference for white skin over darker skin. The results were consistent across all ages, education levels, and income groups. In 2002, another IAT study found that nearly half of all Americans have an implicit association between European American names and pleasant words versus African American names and unpleasant words.

It is worth pointing out that the IAT has been surrounded by controversy since its inception. Many have questioned the validity of the methodology and the subsequent results produced by the test. This does not mean unconscious bias does not exist, only that it is difficult to measure.

Another common means of testing for the presence of unconscious bias is the blind audition. It is most commonly illustrated within the context of auditions for symphony orchestras. Blind auditions have also been used on The Voice, a popular TV show. It involves an audition whereby the identity of the performer is concealed from the listener, so the listener can focus on the quality of the performance and avoid making judgments based on unconscious biases. Research has shown that the people tasked with evaluating the audition were more likely to select a female performer if they were unaware of their gender, whether the evaluator was male or female.

A third way of measuring bias is to simply review real-world outcomes. If there are fewer women in high-ranking positions than would be expected based on their proportion of the population, for example, then it is likely that unconscious bias is having an impact on employment decisions.

Combating the Horn Effect

The horn effect can create a substantial amount of friction in a team-based work environment. Overcoming an unfair, negative perception of someone else can be difficult but that does not mean that it is not worthwhile. There are a number of strategies that can be used to overcome the adverse impacts of the horn effect, including:

- **Seeking feedback**
- **Encouraging conversation**
- **Giving credit when appropriate**
- **Avoid singling people out in a group environment**
- **Offer team-building exercises**
- **Sharing information**
- **Paying attention to body language**

Leaders should make concerted efforts toward maintaining neutrality. When offering feedback or endeavoring to resolve a dispute, leaders should focus on being as diplomatic as possible, avoid favoritism and unconscious biases. It is important to keep in mind that the role of the leadership is to serve the needs of the employees. Leaders facing problems in which they are personally involved should contact the HR department and/or a neutral third party.

This list of steps is not a conclusive, exhaustive account of techniques to combat the horn effect—it is simply meant to serve as a starting point, a means of opening a conversation and developing a personal strategy.

11

Microaggressions

*The war we have to wage today has only one goal
and that is to make the world safe for diversity.*
—U Thant

Bias and prejudice can take many forms. In some cases, words and actions may be overt, intentionally calculated to oppress members of traditionally marginalized groups and remind them of their 'subordinate' social status. However, bias and prejudice can also be less explicit and intentional. Offensive comments, insults, derogatory behaviors and verbal abuse that people from marginalized groups experience on a frequently reoccurring basis are known as microaggressions, whether intentional or unintentional. Some microaggressions may be intentionally designed to escape the attention of outside observers; others may be an unintentional comment from someone with a lack of understanding about the potential of their words to make a harmful impact.

A few interactions that could generally be characterized as

microaggressions could include jokes or informal feedback, even innocent questions. Oftentimes, microaggressions pass unchallenged and/or completely unnoticed. Microaggressions stem from a lack of awareness about the experiences of marginalized groups, unconscious biases and prejudices. In many cases, the microaggression may be so ambiguous that it is simple for the offending party to explain it away or deny it altogether. This adds to the frustration and hurt feelings experienced by the person on the receiving end. Though it was originally used to describe insults and casual degradations aimed at Black Americans, the term microaggression also now refers to derogatory efforts based on an individual's:

- Disability
- Economic status
- Gender identification
- Sexual orientation
- Social class
- Faith or spirituality

Most of the members of marginalized groups have likely experienced microaggressions. The fact that microaggressions typically refer to words and not actions does not mean they are not harmful. The people responsible for committing microaggressions may not be aware of what they are doing, or it may be an explicit, concerted effort aimed at demeaning a minority group and/or reinforcing negative stereotypes.

Origin

The term "microaggression" was first coined by Chester M. Pierce in 1970. A professor at Harvard Medical School, Pierce was an African American with an impressive track record of achievements, including working at the Massachusetts Institute of Technology as a psychiatrist for 25 years. For Pierce, microaggressions were limited to actions and comments directed at African Americans by other racial groups. He contrasted microaggressions with macroaggressions, which could be defined as more overt and violent acts of racism, such as beatings or lynchings.

In 1986, John Dovido and Samuel Gaertner described the concept of aversive racism, in which negative opinions concerning minority groups are reinforced because other groups avoid having any interactions. It was initially coined by Joel Kovel but Dovido and Gaertner furthered the concept. They pointed out that people may be averse to a group because of negative opinions and/or stereotypes; these individuals may overtly state a belief in equal rights while simultaneously making statements or committing actions that are aversively racist in nature.

In 1995, psychologists Claude Steele and Joshua Aronson published a work on stereotype threat, describing it as a type of fear or anxiety surrounding the performance of an action that is typically associated with the negative stereotypes of a person's group. The fear is associated with confirming the negative stereotype through one's actions and/or comments.

Although Pierce coined the term microaggression, Derald Wing Sue was the main individual responsible for making the term more widespread. For Sue, microaggressions could be defined as a frequent though brief occurrence, in which members of marginalized groups are demeaned through offensive actions and/or comments. In 2007, he co-wrote a work with several other psychologists discussing how racism has evolved over time, as social pressures and norms had moved people away from overtly racist acts to less explicit actions, including aversive racism and microaggressions.

Kevin Nadal has been writing about the impact of microaggressions on traditionally marginalized groups since the early 2010s. He got his start as a social activist by launching an online petition against the TV show Desperate Housewives for making derogatory statements about medical schools in the Philippines, in 2007. Since then Nadal has written extensively on the importance of stopping bullies in the school system, the ways that LGBTQ people experience microaggressions, colorism, the marginalization of Filipino Americans and other Asian Americans of darker complexion, and why homophobic and transphobic beliefs should be challenged.

Microaggressions

Sue and his peers wrote in 2007 that there are three types of microaggressions: microassaults, microinsults and microinvalidations.

Microassaults

Microassaults tend to be more obvious and deliberate. Whether verbal or nonverbal, microassaults represent an action that is explicit and racially motivated. Calling someone a name, avoiding the members of a marginalized group, and intentionally discriminating against people are all examples of microassaults.

Microinsults

These microaggressions could be defined as a comment with a concealed insult that is either rude or insensitive. In most cases, the derogatory comment made by the communicator is unintentional; a microinsult is more subtle than a microassault.

Microinvalidations

This refers to a form of microaggression that seeks to nullify the experiences, opinions, feelings or thoughts of a marginalized group. As the name implies, microinvalidations are subtle comments focused on negating, excluding or invalidating the beliefs and thoughts that are important to others.

Impact of Microaggressions

The concept of microaggressions has been criticized extensively. Most of the criticism is centered on the collection methodology and the fact that the data is subjective. For the most part, even the most vocal critics do not dispute the fact that microaggressions exist or that they cause harm to the person on the receiving end.

In his article from 2021, Microaggressions: Death by a Thousand Cuts, Sue argued that microaggressions can have a cumulative effect. Sue, who is a second generation Asian American, used a number of personal experiences to illustrate the concept of microaggressions. One is that he continually receives compliments for speaking 'good' English. Another example Sue provided was the fact that, when boarding crowded subway trains, he noticed that there would usually be an open seat available beside a Black passenger.

Sue believed that people are mostly well-intentioned but the slights, comments and insults they make add up, causing extensive damage to the listener. He wrote that the people who are committing microaggressions were unlikely to have thought about the potential impact of their words. For Sue, microaggressions are rooted in unconscious bias and it is impossible for most people to escape the influence of the biases that are embraced by the broader society.

Sue wrote that, although some critics view the concept of microaggressions as essentially making trouble out of something that was small and insignificant, the fact that microaggressions are a consistent aspect of daily life for people of color results in a cumulative effect. This makes the person on the receiving end lose energy in what Sue terms as 'racial battle fatigue.' Additionally, he believed that microaggressions lower self-esteem, increase stress, impair mental health, add to feelings of depression, decrease problem-solving skills, and create an obstacle to learning new things. Sue also referenced data pointing to how microaggressions can lower the standard of living for people of marginalized groups.

Sue used the cliché about how "sticks and stones may break my bones but words will never hurt me" to illustrate that critics downplay the significance of microaggressions. He wrote that since microaggressions are just words, some critics dispute the significance of microaggressions and their ability to cause harm. In the article, however, Sue pointed out that there is a significant body of research that is contrary to this claim.

Criticism of Microaggression Concept

One of the most vocal critics of the concept of microaggressions was Scott Lilienfeld. He felt that the term microassault should be removed from the cultural lexicon because the actions and comments presented in the definition were far from being 'micro' in nature. Instead, Lilienfeld believed that microassaults actually constituted outright assaults, harassment and other actions aimed at intimidating the recipient. He also felt the word 'aggression' should be removed from the term microaggression, believing its inclusion to be misleading.

Thus, many of Lilienfeld's objections to the concepts were based on semantics. He did argue, however, that the concept did not have the adequate methodology to have a real-world application. Lilienfeld was a psychology professor at Emory University and the co-author of 50 Great Myths of Popular Psychology, a guide book to critical thinking on the subject, so it is easy to see why he would have issues over semantics and methodological practices. Though one of the most prominent and vocal critics of the concept of microaggressions, he wrote that, regardless of how microaggressions are conceptualized, a discussion of them is valid for both universities and businesses. Further, Lilienfeld believed that the people experiencing microaggressions were genuinely offended and that everyone should listen to the concerns of others with an open mind.

Other critics have argued that the term increases the psychological fragility of some individuals, creating a culture of victimhood. Jonathan Haidt, a professor of Ethical Leadership at New York University, wrote that the danger of creating this type of culture is that it reduces a person's ability to navigate small issues without assistance and results in a society where intense moral conflict becomes commonplace. John McWhorter V, an associate professor of Linguistics at Columbia University, has a similar viewpoint. In an article that was published in The American Interest in 2018, he wrote that, "It infantilizes Black people to be taught that microaggressions, and even ones a tad more macro, hold us back, permanently damage our psychology, or render us exempt from genuine competition."

McWhorter also wrote that focusing on microaggressions too much had the potential to cause other problems. According to Haidt, who wrote an article in The Atlantic along with Greg Lukianoff, a problem that could arise from too much focus on microaggressions would be that doing so could cause more harm than the occurrence. In regard to an academic setting where preventative programs exist to reduce microaggressions, Lukianoff and Haidt argued that too much focus on the concept would impede a person's ability to have intellectual discussions with other people they disagree with about a number of topics. Similarly, other critics have argued that it inhibits the willingness of societal participants to engage in free speech.

Regardless of whether these criticisms are valid, there is very little disagreement about the existence of microaggressions. It is also worth noting that there is little disagreement about the psychological harm that microaggressions can cause. Sue's work provides a guide for navigating these issues, as he argued that his intent in popularizing the term was not motivated by a desire to silence people or make them feel ashamed. His goal was simply to educate people about the issue and he did not believe that everyone who had committed a microaggression was a racist. Similar to Lilienfeld, who wrote that people should be open about the idea that they have been insensitive, Sue believed that a discussion of microaggressions should utilize a collaborative approach instead of something accusatory and/or argumentative.

Many have pointed out that microaggressions exist because societal norms and evolving ideas centered on equality have made overtly racist acts more unacceptable. Microaggressions are obviously terrible but if there is a silver lining it is that society has moved toward a place that is more accepting and enlightened. The way to move forward is to eliminate the unconscious beliefs and biases that result in microaggressions, but how is it possible to make that happen?

One way to reduce the impact of unconscious bias is to simply make an effort to get to know people from other groups. Aversive racism is real and it has a tendency to be self-reinforcing. Taking the time to learn about other cultures can be a positive step. Likewise, reading about other cultures, religions and countries can help to eliminate unconscious biases. Traveling can have a similar positive impact in terms of its potential to expand individual perceptions, beliefs and opinions.

As Sue points out, it is important to remember that words have value and, although they may not be sticks and stones, that does not mean they do not have the ability to make a harmful impact. To move forward, people should carefully review their words before speaking. Everyone makes mistakes; however, through education, open dialogue and a little careful consideration, there is an opportunity to decrease the number of mistakes and move society to a better place.

12

Discrimination in the Workplace

*"Discrimination is hated, and there is no place
for it in the workplace. Strive to be a person
or organization who promotes diversity and
commits to sustaining an inclusive culture."*

—Germany Kent

A workplace free of harassment and discrimination is a right that every employee deserves. Most discriminatory practices originate from unconscious and conscious biases, prejudices and stereotypes. As a result, minorities and other historically marginalized groups are the most at risk for experiencing discrimination in the workplace.

In the US, employees who are a part of a protected class such as age, race, ethnicity, national origin, sex, disability, or religion have legal rights not to be harassed at work. Unfortunately, it is not uncommon for American workers to face discriminatory practices in the workplace on a variety of fronts, despite legal protections under a series of anti-discrimination laws.

Workplace discrimination is an act that violates equal employment opportunity laws. These laws were created to prevent employers from unjustly discriminating against employees based on certain characteristics. While most anti-discrimination laws specifically apply to employers with at least 15 employees, some apply to smaller companies as well. For example, sexual harassment claims can be brought against employers with less than 15 employees.

It's important for workers to know their rights in regard to discrimination in the workplace. With that in mind, the following is intended to provide an overview of major Federal anti-discrimination laws and how they protect workers from unfair treatment on the job.

Employees are protected from discrimination by the Civil Rights Act of 1964. The Act prohibits discrimination based on race, color, religion, sex, or national origin. It also prohibits retaliation for filing a discrimination complaint or participating in an investigation related to a complaint.

The Equal Pay Act of 1963 (EPA), as amended, protects men and women who perform substantially equal work in the same establishment from sex-based wage differentials. Under the EPA, employers may not pay unequal wages to men and women who perform jobs that require substantially equal skill, effort, and responsibility under similar working conditions within the same establishment.

The Pregnancy Discrimination Act of 1978 prohibits employers from discriminating against workers because they are pregnant or have recently given birth. Employers must provide accommodations such as more frequent breaks and more time off to pregnant workers if they provide similar accommodations to other workers who need it due to medical conditions.

The Age Discrimination in Employment Act of 1967 protects employees age 40 and older from discrimination on the basis of age. It also prohibits retaliating against an employee for filing a complaint regarding age discrimination.

Title I and Title V of the Americans with Disabilities Act of 1990 prohibit employment discrimination against qualified individuals with disabilities in the private sector and in state and local governments.

Many people often confuse harassment with discrimination, and although there are similarities between the two, there are also some key differences. Harassment is illegal and is a violation of Federal law. Discrimination is also illegal, though it is not a criminal offense. Although often used interchangeably, the terms have different meanings. It is important to understand the differences because the law treats harassment and discrimination differently.

Discrimination occurs when a person is treated less favorably than another person in a similar situation because of a protected attribute (such as race, sex, or disability). Discrimination can occur on its own, or it can result from the application of neutral rules and policies that adversely affect people with a particular attribute.

On the other hand, harassment is a type of employment discrimination that involves unwanted or inappropriate behavior in the workplace. The behavior can be directed at an employee based on race, gender, disability, or other protected class.

Unwelcome conduct may include offensive remarks about a person's protected status. The law doesn't prohibit simple teasing, offhand comments or isolated incidents that are not very serious. Harassment becomes illegal, however, when it is so frequent or severe that it creates a hostile or offensive work environment, or when it results in an adverse employment decision. The following includes an analysis of the different forms of discrimination and harassment.

Discrimination

The term "discrimination" means to distinguish, single out, or make a distinction between persons or things on the basis of a class or category. It occurs when implicit biases, prejudices (personal and institutional), and stereotypes lead to various forms of unfair treatment. Unfair treatment could result from hiring practices, promotions, job assignments, terminations, and levels of compensation. Unfair treatment claims could also result from unfair allocation of resources, denial of access, social exclusion, and various forms of harassment.

In the context of employment, the law defines discrimination as any unfavorable treatment based on several characteristics, including but not limited to, race, sex, age, color, national origin, religion, disability, or pregnancy.

Discrimination can take many forms—it doesn't have to be blatant or intentional. In fact, it may be more subtle and go unnoticed by others. It can be as obvious as someone saying something inappropriate or racist in the workplace. Significantly, discrimination could also be as simple as an employer only inviting younger employees to social gatherings after work (age discrimination).

There are two main types of employment discrimination: disparate treatment and disparate impact. Disparate treatment involves a policy or practice that treats some people less favorably than others because of a protected characteristic. An example would be if an employer gave all female employees lower performance reviews than male employees simply because of their gender.

Disparate impact occurs when an employer's policy or practice as an adverse effect on members of a protected class. The difference is that the policy or practice may appear to be neutral. If it is found that there is no legitimate business reason for the policy or practice, and it is negatively impactful to certain individuals and/or groups, then it's likely the policy/practice is having a disparate impact. For example, if a company only hires people who speak English fluently and this requirement has a negative effect on people of a particular nationality, it may be discriminatory unless speaking English in the workplace was necessary for business purposes.

Caroline King, PhD

Harassment

When it comes to defining harassment, the line is often blurred between what is regarded as acceptable and what is regarded as unacceptable. It is not uncommon for sexual harassment and gender discrimination to be depicted on TV and in the movies. The media is at least partially responsible for how the definition of what is and is not acceptable has evolved over the years. This is not to downplay how society has moved toward a place of more acceptance and equality over the years. One example of the shift in prevailing attitudes could be provided by viewing the TV show, "Mad Men." Some behaviors that were acceptable in the past are now considered taboo, for good reason.

What many fail to realize is that harassment is not only limited to two forms of discrimination. Instead, harassment can take many forms. The following is intended as an overview of the various types of harassment one may commonly find in the workplace.

Verbal harassment – This is the most common form of workplace harassment. Verbal abuse can take many different forms, such as slurs, derogatory comments, or insults about a person's race, ethnicity, sex, age, disability, and other such characteristics.

Physical harassment – Although physical acts of violence only make up a small percentage of reported cases of workplace harassment, the repercussions can obviously have a significant impact on both the individual and the organization. Also, it is worth noting that physical harassment can include unwanted touching, threats of violence and physically intimidating behaviors.

Quid Pro Quo harassment – This form of harassment refers to a 'this for that' exchange, such as when a job, promotion or benefit is conditioned on an employee submitting to unwelcome sexual advances. An example would be if an employee was denied a promotion unless she went on a date with her boss.

Visual harassment – Any sort of image or display that is harassing in nature could be considered workplace harassment. Examples could include lewd pictures and racially offensive symbols.

Sexual harassment – This form of harassment refers to unwanted sexual advances, sexual jokes/remarks, or any other sexually-oriented behavior that creates a hostile work environment.

Gender-based harassment – Both men and women may be harassed because of nonconformance to traditional gender roles. However, this type of harassment is more frequently aimed at women.

Racial and ethnic harassment – This form of harassment includes offensive comments about minorities, slurs, derogatory statements about cultural differences, or jokes regarding someone's accent.

Religious harassment – This form of harassment involves comments or actions focus on deriding an individual's spiritual beliefs and/or practices.

Disability-related harassment – This type of harassment occurs when an employee with mental or physical impairments is harassed.

Microaggressions/micro-assaults – This refers to a comment, intentional or unintentional, that appears non-substantial on the surface. As previously mentioned, microaggressions can have significant, negative impact.

Retaliation harassment – This type of harassment refers to a comment or action taken against an employee who reported another form of harassment. Retaliation is taken very seriously in statutory and common law jurisdictions since it potentially undermines the core purpose of anti-discrimination statutes, which is preventing future discrimination. Employees dealing with retaliation should be sure to make reports early, accurately, and whenever possible, in writing. Individuals experiencing retaliation in the workplace should immediately contact the EEOC.

Financial Costs of Discrimination and Harassment

The costs associated with harassment and discrimination in the workplace can be difficult to quantify. Some costs, of course, are relatively easy to assess, such as lost productivity, legal fees and medical expenses. Harassment and discrimination can impact many aspects of the organization, creating a ripple effect that makes the costs more difficult to measure. A few of these would include low employee morale, customer dissatisfaction, and loss of reputation. The following is intended as an overview of the various costs that can result from harassment and discrimination.

Productivity losses – A harassment or discrimination claim can have a significant impact on every organizational level. When people do not feel as if their contributions are going to be valued or if the workplace environment is toxic, it is unlikely they will apply their best effort or come together in support of the organizational mission.

Employee turnover – In a workplace that is characterized by harassment and/or discriminatory processes/practices, there is likely to be a high turnover rate. Similar to productivity losses, employees are unlikely to buy into the organizational mission if the workplace environment is toxic. Claims associated with harassment and discrimination can therefore dramatically increase the costs associated with recruitment and retention.

Employee absenteeism – Absences can have a direct, measurable impact on productivity, as well as a more indirect impact on the morale of the employees left behind to pick up the slack. This can make the financial burden associated with harassment and discrimination more difficult to quantify.

Decreased employee morale – Workplace harassment affects employee morale and makes workers feel less engaged with their jobs. They may become dissatisfied with their jobs and start looking for something new for the simple fact it is easier to work somewhere with a positive environment. Organizations that turn a blind eye to harassment and discrimination risk losing key employees.

Legal risks – Organizations can be exposed to a variety of legal risks if claims associated with harassment and discrimination are not investigated in a timely manner. Discriminatory practices and retaliatory actions against reporting employees can also bring a variety of costs, including penalties and attorney fees. The following includes a list of behaviors that could be considered as harassment:

- **Offensive jokes**
- **Slurs**
- **Intimidation or threats**
- **Ridicule or mockery**
- **Making derogatory comments**
- **Offensive objects or pictures**
- **Interference with work performance**
- **Offensive gestures**

Having to go to work can feel like a punishment in itself sometimes. Having to go to work in a toxic environment, of course, is only going to make things worse. For those who are in the unfortunate position of having to deal with harassment and/or discrimination in the workplace, there is a clear process to follow in the interest of safeguarding best interests and holding the people responsible accountable for their actions.

1. Keep a detailed account of all of the events that transpired, including names and dates.
2. Notify HR and/or the relevant supervisor, preferably in writing.
3. Gather witnesses and/or other victims if possible.
4. Follow up the relevant HR professional and/or supervisor to ensure the appropriate action was taken, in writing.
5. File a complaint with the EEOC.
6. If the EEOC does not consider it to be a valid claim and elects not to assign an attorney to the case, consider whether or not it will be beneficial to talk to an attorney and file a private lawsuit.

Steps six and seven should only be considered if the appropriate action is not taken by the employer.

While it is impossible to know exactly how many people are experiencing harassment or discrimination in the workplace, as there are many unreported instances of both, there are no shortage of resources available related to how to deal with harassment or discrimination.

Certain company policies and procedures can help protect employees from harassment. These could include having a non-discriminatory hiring process, clear company expectations, and professional training for all employees. This can help employees gain an understanding of company expectations and learn how to handle these types of situations if they occur.

Ultimately, the goal is to create a culture of respect where everyone understands that harassment and discrimination are not going to be tolerated. Aside from being the right thing to do, eliminating harassment and discrimination can also reduce organizational costs. The first step toward achieving that goal is to create an employee handbook and set clear expectations, so everyone knows what kind of behavior is acceptable at work.

13

Assimilation

"There is this myth, that America is a melting pot,
but what happens in assimilation is that we end up
deliberately choosing the American things - hot dogs
and apple pie - and ignoring the Chinese offerings."
—Amy Tan

Cultural assimilation occurs when an ethic minority sacrifices its own culture to integrate into society, Cultural assimilation believes in

a homogenous, rather than a diverse society. The rate of immigration to the United States quadrupled after 1970 and doubled after 1990.The world we live in is better connected today than ever before. Globalization and modern technology have enabled many individuals to move to different countries and settle in, leading to increased cultural assimilation. As a result of this assimilation, many people are foregoing their own culture - language, religion, customs and traditions - in order to fit in with the majority population. This is particularly true for immigrants coming into societies that have a dominant influence, such as the United States. The rate of cultural assimilation is further accelerated by economic factors, with many individuals seeking to improve their economic well-being by altering their lifestyles and values in order to be accepted into the wider society. Although this process can lead to increased social cohesion, it may also lead to a loss of identity for the minority group if it is not recognized and appreciated by the larger society. It is therefore important to create an inclusive environment where all cultures are respected, regardless of their differences. This can be done through programs such as cultural education, dialogue and understanding, civil engagement initiatives, and other policies that promote mutual respect between different communities. By recognizing each individual's cultural heritage, we can ensure that cultural assimilation does not lead to the erasure of important identities and traditions. In this way, we can foster a more harmonious society where all people are respected and accepted.

We can also create an environment in which diversity is encouraged. This means celebrating and respecting differences between cultures by preserving the language and customs of minority groups. This can be done by providing educational opportunities, government funding for cultural events, and other initiatives that promote the preservation of heritage languages and cultures. It is also important to create economic opportunities for members of minority communities, so they can participate meaningfully in society without having to sacrifice their own culture in order to do so. Good examples of these initiatives are the ones being taken by many cities and states in the U.S., such as providing language courses and job training programs, or hosting events that highlight different cultures and create a platform for cultural exchange. Only through understanding, tolerance, and acceptance can we truly build an inclusive society that respects each other's differences.

By understanding and promoting cultural assimilation as a positive way of social integration, we can create a more cohesive society where everyone has the opportunity to achieve their full

potential while still able to maintain their own culture. This will not only benefit individuals but also contribute to a better future for our global society.

Cultural Assimilation Definition

Cultural assimilation is the process by which a person or group of people adopt the customs, attitudes and behaviors of another culture. It occurs when individuals from minority cultures become part of majority cultures, often losing their own cultural identities in the process. Cultural assimilation can happen through contact between cultures and societies, either through migration or intermarriage. When it happens gradually over time, it can be seen as a natural consequence of living among different groups. However, it can also be forced upon individuals and groups as a result of discrimination or oppression.

Assimilation has both positive and negative effects on both majority and minority populations. On one hand, it can provide opportunities for better access to resources such as education and employment that may have been previously denied to minority groups. On the other hand, it can lead to a loss of cultural identity and may even be used as a tool for oppression by those in power. When this happens, assimilation can cause disruption in both social and economic systems and can create tension between different cultures.

Cultural assimilation is an ongoing process that has occurred throughout history. It continues to shape our society today, and its effects are significant. By understanding the effects of cultural assimilation, we can strive towards more equitable societies where all cultures are respected and upheld. As different cultures come into contact with each other, it is important to recognize the need for respect and understanding between them in order to ensure a more harmonious future.

It is essential that those who experience cultural assimilation feel empowered to maintain their heritage and pass it on to future generations. This will allow them to feel connected to their past while also being able to embrace new opportunities without sacrificing their cultural roots.

Cultural assimilation can be beneficial when done in an equitable way that preserves the unique heritage and identity of all involved. By working together, we can create a society where everyone's culture is celebrated and honored.

Historical Assimilation of Immigrants

Immigration to the United States has caused a diverse assimilation of cultures and values, making it one of the most culturally-rich countries in the world. As immigrants have come from different parts of the world, they have brought with them their own sets of beliefs and traditions, which sometimes clash with those of American culture. Assimilation is defined as the adoption of certain practices by an immigrant group into mainstream society, often through socialization over time.

The process of assimilation for immigrants has varied greatly over time. In earlier years, assimilation was often seen as something that required individuals to "lose" their identity and traditions in order to fit in. This could be done by speaking English or taking on characteristics associated with the dominant American culture. Today, the process of assimilation has shifted to one of integration, where immigrants are able to retain their identity while still adapting to their new home.

Historically, assimilation of immigrants has been a difficult but ultimately beneficial process. Cultural differences present challenges at times, yet they can also bring out aspects in both cultures that otherwise would have remained unknown or overlooked. As such, it is important that these differences be recognized and celebrated as part of what makes up a truly diverse society. This may take time and an effort on everyone's part, but ultimately it will lead to a better understanding of different cultures and more meaningful interactions between groups.

Today, immigration continues to shape who we are as Americans. Immigrants have always been a part of this country's history and they will continue to be in the future. As such, it is important to recognize the importance of assimilation and integration, so that immigrants can retain their identities while also becoming integrated into American society.

By doing so, we ensure that our cultural identity remains strong and vibrant for generations to come. This is how we honor our past, present, and future immigrants – by recognizing their contributions and creating an environment where all cultures are respected. In this way, we honor the spirit of America: one nation with many stories. Together, we form a unique tapestry of cultures that make up this great land. This is what makes America beautiful. Together, we can all contribute to a brighter future for everyone.

The assimilation process of immigrants is one that must be both accepted and celebrated in order to ensure cultural diversity and integration into American society. It takes time and effort from all involved, but ultimately the benefits are well worth it. By understanding and accepting different cultures, we foster respect within our communities and create a stronger nation as a whole. This will enable us to form meaningful relationships with individuals who come from unique backgrounds, appreciate their contributions to our society, and build bridges that unite us all.

Immigrants arriving at Ellis Island in the early 1900s. Photo Credit: National Park Service

Leah Boustan of UCLA, and Katherine Eriksson of UC Davis have done extensive research on historical assimilation known as the Age of Mass Migration from 1850 to 1913, when U.S. borders were open and 30 million Europeans picked up stakes to move here. By the early 20th century, some 15 percent of the U.S. population was foreign born, comparable to the share today. If we want to we come in warranty society we must look to the lessons of the past but not repeat or mistakes.

Leah Boustan and Katherine Eriksson's research on the Age of Mass Migration serves as an important reminder that immigrants have been a vital part of American society for centuries. We must not forget the lessons of the past, while also recognizing that our approach to immigration today needs to be different.

Immigrants have traditionally enriched our nation in countless ways, and it is important that we recognize and embrace the positive contributions they make. Today, immigration policies should be crafted to ensure that all immigrants have equal access to opportunities for success – whether through legal pathways or other programs that guarantee civil rights and humanitarian protection. We must guard against repeating the mistakes of our past while also recognizing the potential of immigration to continue helping our nation to thrive.

Immigrants today bring knowledge, skills, and new perspectives which can help us create a stronger economy and vibrant culture. With an open heart and creative spirit, we can work together to create a more inclusive society that welcomes those seeking a better life in the United States. We owe it to ourselves as well as future generations to create policies that will support the growth of a diverse and vibrant American community.

By taking our cue from past wisdom and applying it to today's changing landscape, we can create a better future for all who call the United States home. By doing so, we can ensure that immigrants are met with acceptance rather than hostility and that they are given access to the same opportunities as native-born Americans. We must move away from fear-based policies and instead embrace an approach of respect, fairness, and inclusivity in order to create a more equitable society for all. Through this unified effort, we can honor the legacy of those who have come before us, while creating new opportunities for ourselves and future generations.

By learning from the past, we can create better immigration policies for tomorrow. Only then can we create a society that is truly inclusive and welcoming of all who seek to make a life in America.

The research conducted by Leah Boustan and Katherine Eriksson highlights the long history of immigration in our country and its potential to benefit everyone. We must learn from the successes and failures of the past to ensure that immigrants today have access to opportunities for success without fear or prejudice. By creating fair, equitable policies that recognize the value of immigration and its contributions to our nation, we can move toward a future where every individual has an equal chance at achieving their dreams. By understanding our shared history, celebrating diversity, and creating inclusive policies, we can create a better future for all.

Our key finding is that for immigrants who arrived in the 1900s and 1910s, the more time they spent in the U.S., the less likely they were to give their children foreign-sounding names. Figure 1 shows that after 20 years in this country, half of the gap in name choice between immigrants and natives had disappeared. The shift in name choice happened at a roughly equal pace for sons and daughters and among poor and rich families.

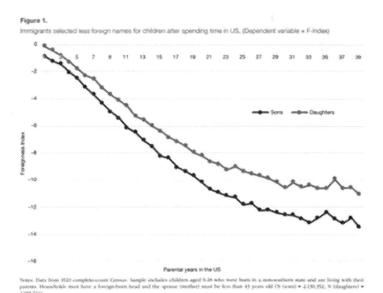

Figure 1.
Immigrants selected less foreign names for children after spending time in US. (Dependent variable = F-index)

However, the pace varied significantly depending on country of origin. Immigrants from Norway, Sweden, and Denmark were among the quickest to adopt American-sounding names, followed by Italians and other Southern Europeans. Russians, including many Russian Jews, and Finns had the slowest rates of name-based assimilation. This convergence of names chosen by immigrant and native populations is suggestive evidence of cultural assimilation. But the fact that immigrants didn't fully adopt native naming patterns suggests that many valued retaining a distinct cultural identity.

Having an American-sounding name was a badge of assimilation that conferred genuine economic and social benefits. We looked at census records of more than a million children of immigrants from 1920, when they lived with their childhood families, through 1940, when they were adults.

Children with less-foreign-sounding names completed more years of schooling, earned more, and were less likely to be unemployed than their counterparts whose names sounded more foreign. In addition, they were less likely to marry someone born abroad or with a foreign-sounding name. These patterns held even among brothers within the same family. The data suggest that, while a foreign-sounding name reinforced a sense of ethnic identity, it may have exposed individuals to discrimination at school or on the job.

Other measures reinforce the picture of early 20th century immigrants gradually taking on American cultural markers. By 1930, more than two-thirds of immigrants had applied for citizenship and almost all reported they could speak some English. A third of first-generation immigrants who arrived unmarried, and more than half of second-generation immigrants wed spouses from outside their cultural group.

These findings suggest that over time immigrants' sense of separateness weakened and their identification with U.S. culture grew stronger. The gradual adoption of American-sounding names appears to have been part of a process of assimilation in which newcomers learned U.S. culture, made a commitment to build roots in this country, and came to identify as Americans.

Some may have arrived with a strong desire to assimilate, but little knowledge of how to do so. They may not even have known which names were common in the U.S. Others may not have cared about assimilating at first, but eventually felt the urge to blend in. In both cases, as time went by, they may have started to navigate the dominant culture with greater ease. Their children may have attended schools with children from other cultures and have spoken with American accents.

What does this tell us about the assimilation process? We can imagine that after many years in the U.S., immigrants, like natives, become baseball fans, eat hamburgers, and watch fireworks on the Fourth of July. To be sure, their connections with their countries of origin are not obliterated. Instead, they may come to see themselves as hyphenated Americans, but Americans nonetheless.

This study provides important insights into the relationship between assimilation and cultural identity in an immigrant context. It highlights the complex dynamics at play when immigrants choose to adopt new naming practices while also wanting to preserve their own cultures. By understanding the complexities of assimilation, we can create policies that best support immigrants in adapting to their new home cultures while preserving their own cultural identities and fostering successful integration into host countries.

The findings from this study suggest that having an American-sounding name does not necessarily mean full assimilation, as it is only one part of a complicated process. This information is essential for creating effective policies that foster successful assimilation among immigrant populations. Policymakers should take these complexities into account when creating such policies, which are key to supporting immigrants in succeeding in their new. This research provides evidence for the complex dynamics between assimilation and cultural identity for immigrant populations. It highlights how policymakers must

Immigrants from Norway, Sweden, and Denmark were the quickest to adopt American-sounding names, reflecting their relatively smooth transition into the culture. Italians and other Southern Europeans followed close behind in terms of name-based assimilation. On the other hand, Russians and Finns had a much slower rate of name adoption due to a desire to retain their distinct cultural identity. This is evident in that even when immigrants began using more "American" sounding names, they still often did not completely conform to native naming patterns - suggesting an attachment to their own culture even as they adapted to new norms.

The fact that immigrants took steps towards adopting native naming practices shows that there was indeed some level of cultural assimilation taking place. However, this slow rate of name adoption reflects the fact that immigrants valued keeping their own cultural identity - sometimes even at the expense of complete assimilation. This is an important part of understanding immigration patterns and demonstrates the complicated relationship between assimilation and maintaining distinct cultural identities.

This study shows that having an American-sounding name does confer some economic and social benefits, but is not a guarantee of complete assimilation. While some immigrants may adopt native naming practices as part of their journey towards full integration into the culture, others may choose to maintain distinct cultural identities even while adapting to the new society. Either way, it is clear that this process is complex and should be taken into account when studying immigration patterns and assimilation.

Overall, this study highlights the importance of understanding the nuances of immigrant experiences in order to properly assess their level of assimilation and success with integrating into their new home culture. The fact that immigrants take steps towards adopting native naming practices shows that there is indeed some level of cultural assimilation taking place - even if it is a slow process. Understanding these complexities can help us to have more accurate and nuanced views of the immigration experience.

By understanding this complexity, we can gain a better understanding of how immigrants navigate the journey towards full integration into their new home cultures. We can also identify policy measures that can help promote successful assimilation, which is beneficial for both immigrants and their host countries.

This study provides important insights into the relationship between assimilation and cultural identity in an immigrant context. It highlights the complex dynamics at play when immigrants choose to adopt new naming practices while also wanting to retain their own distinct cultures. Understanding this complexity can help us gain a better understanding of how immigrants navigate the journey towards full integration into their new home cultures, as well as identify policy measures that can help promote successful assimilation for both immigrants and their host countries. This information is essential for creating policies that best support immigrant populations in succeeding in their new homes.

The findings from this study suggest that immigrants' sense of separateness is weakening and their identification with U.S. culture is growing stronger as they gradually adopt American-sounding names. This process, however, is complex and slow, suggesting that immigrants are still attached to their own cultural identity even while adapting to new norms. Policymakers should take into account this complexity when seeking to foster successful assimilation for immigrant populations in order to create policies that best support them in succeeding in their new homes.

Overall, this study is an important contribution to the conversation on immigration and assimilation. It shows that having an American-sounding name does not necessarily mean full assimilation, as it is only one part of a complicated process. The findings suggest that immigrants are taking steps towards adopting native naming practices but still maintaining their distinct cultural identities. Understanding these complexities can help create policies that best support immigrants in adapting to their new homes while also preserving their own cultures. This information is essential for fostering successful integration into host countries.

This study provides an important contribution to the conversation on immigration and assimilation. It shows that having an American-sounding name does not necessarily mean full assimilation, as it is only one part of a complicated process. By understanding these complexities, policymakers can create policies that best support immigrants in adapting to their new homes while preserving their own cultures and fostering successful integration into host countries. This information is essential for creating policies that foster successful assimilation for immigrant populations.

In conclusion, this study highlights the complexity of the assimilation process for immigrants. It suggests that having an American-sounding name does not necessarily mean full assimilation, as it is only one part of a complicated process. In order to create policies that best support immigrants in adapting to their new homes while preserving their own cultures and fostering successful integration into host countries, policymakers should take this complexity into account. This information is essential for creating effective policies that foster successful assimilation among immigrant populations.

By understanding the complexities of assimilation, we can create policies that best support immigrants in adapting to their new home cultures while preserving their own cultural identities and fostering successful integration into host countries. The findings from this study provide an important contribution to the conversation on immigration and assimilation. They suggest that having an American-sounding name does not necessarily mean full assimilation, as it is only one part of a complicated process. Policymakers should take these complexities into account when creating effective policies that foster successful assimilation among immigrant populations. This information is essential for creating policies that best support immigrants in succeeding in their new homes.

Historical Global Assimilation Example

Native Americans

The first attempts towards cultural assimilation of the Native Americans were seen in the 16th century with the arrival of European colonizers in America. The Spaniards began a program called the 'Encomienda System', to educate the natives in European customs and convert them to Christianity, while using them for labor. Later, the US government started a forced assimilation program in the 19th and early 20th centuries, wherein the Indians were forbidden from practicing their traditional ceremonies, and were compelled to give up their land, and attend public school and church. The impact it had on native culture can be seen by the fact that, as of 2014, only about 154 languages of the erstwhile 300 were being spoken.

European Immigrants to America

When the US was founded, 4 out of every 5 citizens belonged to the White Anglo-Saxon Protestant (WASP) group of North European ancestry. The first immigrants following independence were Germans, Scandinavians, and other people from North and Western Europe. Being well-educated, skilled, and of similar heritage, these immigrants were quickly assimilated into American society. However, later immigrants were from South and East Europe, such as the Polish and Italians, who were considered racially and culturally inferior by the WASP group, and, as a result, had trouble integrating into the mainstream. These immigrants were Catholics, as opposed to the Protestant orientation of the WASP group, and were less-educated or skilled, making them seem undesirable. After a controversial assimilation policy, where these immigrants were encouraged to sacrifice their roots, they had largely been assimilated by the mid-20th century.

Asian Immigration to Developed Countries

After the mid-20th century, developed countries like the UK and USA have seen increasing waves of Asian immigrants. Most of these come from countries such as China, India, Pakistan, and Bangladesh. While the recent rise in religious extremism has focused attention on immigrants from the latter two countries, studies from the UK indicate that Asian immigrants are, in fact, the most ready to assimilate into British society, even compared to immigrants from the United States, Italy, and Ireland.

Australian Aborigines

Australia was inhabited by natives called aborigines long before the arrival of the Europeans. These tribes have faced explicit discrimination since then, having their lands usurped by settlers, after which they were forced into cities where they were considered inferior to the whites, and segregated. After the end of World War II, the government began issuing certificates to those aborigines who wished to be treated as equal citizens. However, to obtain this 'exemption' certificate, an individual had to break off all ties with his community, and even his own family. In effect, this policy encouraged aborigines to adopt a Western standard of living in order to improve their dismal living conditions.

Spanish Inquisition

When Spain reconquered the Iberian Peninsula from the Moors in the 15th century, it began enforcing the Catholic religion. These Moors were Muslim invaders who had ruled the peninsula for more than 700 years. This period saw an increase in the number of converts to Judaism and Islam. The following inquisition ordered all these converts to either return to Catholicism or leave the country. By doing this, the Spanish Crown aimed to destroy opposition and punish any dissenters who

might destabilize the kingdom from within. To avoid persecution, many converts officially reconverted to Catholicism, but continued to practice their old religion in secrecy. The inquisition continued right until the mid-19th century, when it was abandoned by the Crown.

West Indies

The West Indies was colonized by Europeans beginning in the 17th century, after overthrowing the indigenous Arawak Indians. The resulting infrastructure of the colony, first used by the White colonizers, and then by the Africans, was strongly European in nature, with some influences of the local culture. Later, with the arrival of more Europeans, Asians, and Africans, more cultural elements were added to West Indian society. One characteristic feature of West Indian culture was that, though various societies gave their own contributions to it, these were slowly assimilated into the native society. As a result, modern West Indies has a population of mixed ancestry, but its culture is distinctly Creole (influenced by natives).

The ideology of cultural assimilation has a controversial reputation, especially because it believes in a comparison between cultures. Each time an individual or group from a minority community lose their culture to a dominant community, the world is robbed of a trove of cultural wealth that may be several centuries old. This also takes away the chance from the dominant community of learning and benefiting from an interesting culture that they have a little chance of encountering in their lives.

Modern day perspective on Cultural Assimilation

Today's immigrants differ markedly in ethnicity, education, and occupation from those who came during the Age of Mass Migration. Over the past half century, the U.S. has experienced a second wave of mass migration with characteristics that set it apart from what took place in the late 19th and early 20th centuries.

The contemporary migration wave is highly regulated, favoring those with money, education, and skills and drawing migrants primarily

from Asia and Latin America. Selection of immigrants today is often positive, meaning those who come here are more highly skilled than their compatriots who stay in their countries of origin. In the past, immigrants were sometimes negatively selected, meaning they were less skilled than those who stayed behind. Finally, legal immigration now is accompanied by a large undocumented inflow, which complicates efforts to study immigration effects (Vasiliki,2015).

Assimilation means absorbing new things into a system. Assimilation is most often talked about in the context of "cultural assimilation," which is when immigrant groups are encouraged to "adopt the culture, values, and social behaviors of their host nation." This means shedding or hiding aspects of one's culture – including certain foods, clothing, language, religious traditions, etc – that the host nation is unfamiliar with. Supporters of assimilation claim it creates a more cohesive cultural identity, reduces cultural conflict, and helps immigrants gain more social and economic opportunities. In this article, we'll discuss the theoretical models of assimilation, as well as what assimilation can look like in practice. Are supporters of assimilation correct in their claims or does assimilation lead to discrimination and cultural destruction?

Cultural assimilation in theory

Cultural assimilation has existed for as long as people have moved from place to place. In a 2018 article on ThoughtCo, Dr. Nicki Lisa Cole describes how sociologists in the US first began developing theories on assimilation early in the 20th century. From their work, three theoretical models of assimilation were developed:

Historical Model

This first model embraces the idea of the US as a melting pot. It presents assimilation as a linear process where each generation becomes more and more similar to the dominant culture. While the children of immigrants may keep some of their parent's traditions, their children (and the children after them) are more likely to lose elements of their grandparents' culture. Eventually, everyone shares the same culture. This theory is not without criticism. It's been called "Anglo-conformist." It also only works if the mainstream, dominant culture is something that's easily defined.

Racial/ethnic Disadvantage

This theory frames assimilation as a process that varies based on factors like race, ethnicity, and religion. Depending on where a person is from, they may enjoy a fairly easy assimilation process, but for others (usually non-White immigrants), racism and xenophobia may make it much more challenging. Learning the language and adhering to the dominant cultural values will not help immigrants facing increased discrimination. There are major personal and societal consequences when some groups are privileged and others are disadvantaged.

Segmented Assimilation

The segmented assimilation model applies to all immigrants, regardless of their ethnicity or origin. Factors such as language proficiency, education level, employment history, and class background determine which parts of society an immigrant is able to access when integrating into a new country. Those with higher educational attainment are more likely to assimilate faster than those with lower levels of education. It is also important to note that immigrants who keep many of their cultural values and traditions may still successfully assimilate into the host culture.

Segmented assimilation has implications for both migrant communities and receiving societies. For migrants, it determines how much they can benefit from their move in terms of economic opportunity, social mobility, and cultural acceptance. For receiving societies, segmented assimilation informs the availability and quality of services available to immigrants and the integration policies needed to foster meaningful inclusion. Understanding segmented assimilation can help governments, organizations, and individuals create a more equitable environment for successful adaptation and involvement in society.

The concept of segmented assimilation is an important one, as it provides insight into how immigrants negotiate their way through different parts of society. By recognizing the different pathways that exist, we can better understand how migration leads to diverse outcomes. It also enables us to identify areas for improvement in terms of support for migrants so they can take full advantage of the opportunities available in their new home country. The implications of this understanding are vast and should be acknowledged by policymakers and researchers alike.

Assimilation in Practice

As the models show, assimilation is a complex topic. In practice, assimilation often happens naturally as people adjust to a new place and their children grow up surrounded by a different culture. However, assimilation also has an insidious history. In many places, indigenous people and immigrants have been subjected to forced assimilation.

Assimilation is also often inseparable from ideas about race and "the other." Here are two examples of assimilation's dark side:

The United States: Asian Americans and the "model minority" paradox

In the early 20th century, immigration from Asia shifted to Japan. The 1920s saw increased hostility towards Japanese immigrants and citizens of Japanese descent living in the US. This culminated in the forced detention of more than 120,000 Japanese Americans during World War II under President Franklin Roosevelt's Executive Order 9066. Most were relocated to camps in California, Idaho, Utah and other states. After the war ended in 1945, many Japanese Americans were able to get back on their feet through hard work and perseverance. This led to a notion of Asian Americans as the "model minority"—a group that was seen as hardworking, successful and well-assimilated into American society. Yet despite this perception of Asian Americans as the model minority, discrimination persists. Asians are still subjected to racial profiling, hate crimes and job discrimination due to their race or ethnicity. Furthermore, despite stereotypes about Asian achievement, studies show that many Asians continue to lag behind other minorities in terms of education and income levels. The "model minority" paradox thus reveals how assimilation has both positive and negative consequences for Asian Americans. On the one hand, it has enabled them to find success in America; on the other, it has led to stereotypes that can limit their opportunities and obscure the reality of discrimination they still face. This paradox highlights the complexities of race and assimilation in America. It also shows that the journey of Asian Americans toward full acceptance and equal treatment remains ongoing.

This paradox continues today as Asians are both celebrated and demonized. During this time of heightened awareness around race and racism, it is important to recognize the unique experiences of Asian Americans and how they have been shaped by a history of racism in the United States. Understanding this complex history is key to dismantling harmful stereotypes and promoting equity for all people in America.

The struggle for Asian Americans is hardly over. It is essential to recognize the systemic racism that continues to impede the progress of Asian Americans and other minority groups in America. Equity and justice can only be achieved if these issues are seen as part of a larger pattern of oppression rather than isolated incidents. As we work towards achieving an equitable society for all, it is important to remember that the journey is a long one—but it starts with recognizing the unique struggles facing different communities and creating change from within. By supporting efforts to dismantle racism and promote equity, we can continue to make progress on this path toward a more inclusive future for all.

Biculturalism: An Alternative to Assimilation

Biculturalism is a viable alternative to assimilation. It acknowledges the importance of cultural differences, allows for identity to remain intact and even celebrated, and provides a way for minority populations to maintain their own culture while also participating in the dominant one. The concept of biculturalism has been gaining traction in recent years as more people recognize its potential benefits. Biculturalism has many advantages when it comes to navigating both cultures, including increased access to resources, greater integration into society, improved communication skills, and a greater understanding of various perspectives. Furthermore, bicultural individuals often report higher satisfaction with their lives than those who have fully assimilated or failed to adopt certain aspects of the dominant culture.

In addition to the individual benefits of biculturalism, it can also have a positive impact on the larger society. This concept appreciates diversity and is more tolerant of others' cultural differences. When different cultures are seen as being complementary rather than mutually exclusive, it can open up new opportunities for collaboration, communication, and problem-solving that may not have existed before. This can lead to greater understanding between different groups and a sense of unity in the face of potential conflict.

Biculturalism is not a perfect solution—it can come with its own set of challenges—but it does provide an alternative to assimilation that allows people to explore their identities without having to completely abandon them. By embracing both cultural backgrounds, people can become more engaged with their communities and make connections that lead to greater understanding, tolerance, and harmony. In short, biculturalism is an important option that should not be overlooked. By recognizing its potential benefits and working together to create a society where people of different backgrounds can coexist peacefully, we can move towards a brighter future for all can experience unique advantages that may not be available to those who fully assimilate. In this way, it can provide a more inclusive and meaningful experience for people of all backgrounds.

Ultimately, embracing biculturalism is a powerful way to honor cultural differences and allow individuals to find their place in society without sacrificing their identity. Biculturalism creates a platform for both cultural understanding and social progress, and it should not be ignored. By fostering an environment where different cultures can interact peacefully and respectfully, we can create a more harmonious future for everyone.

Real world Experiences an Asian American

The idea of a shared Asian American identity has been fraught for about as long as it has existed. How can one term encapsulate the experiences of people with very different ties to dozens of countries? What shared interests bind refugees struggling to make a home in a new land with people whose families have lived in the United States for generations?

During the coronavirus pandemic, though, fear and pain have acted as grim unifying forces. A surge of violence and harassment targeting Asian Americans has shown that America's long history of treating people of Asian descent as foreigners whose belonging is contingent on labor, on cultural assimilation, on perceived success — is far from a relic.

Still, when we asked people to tell us how it feels to be Asian American right now, many said that the past year and a half has been clarifying in other ways. The responses, which have been condensed and edited, came from Asian Americans across the country and from a variety of backgrounds.

We asked respondents what terms they use to identify themselves. In some cases, full names and ages have been withheld because of safety and privacy concerns.

Many said they felt newly visible vulnerable, but also more keenly aware of how they're seen. Some said they felt compelled to speak out against both anti-Asian discrimination and against other forms of racism in their communities.

Some said they yearned to gain access to an American dream without the burden of prejudice, that they wished simply to blend in. Others said they were embracing their Asian heritage after years of feeling like it made them somehow less American.

> "Now, what's embarrassing is that I ever felt that shame about my family's roots," Jenny Wu Donahue, 33, told us.

> I'm married to a Caucasian man and we used to think it's possible for us to belong. Now we don't. Now people look at me differently when I'm alone versus when I'm with him. I don't feel as safe. I carry a passport that says "U.S. citizen" to prove to people that I belong. Though at times I wonder if it's a reminder to myself that I do.
>
> Anh W., 42, Vietnamese American,
> Eden Prairie, Minn.

> I signed my daughter up for a charter school recently. My husband was filling out the forms and he said we could only choose one ethnicity for my daughter. So he chose white and he didn't choose Asian. I have misgivings about that. But we only had one choice. And I thought, well, she's growing up in the U.S. I guess she is more white now than she is Asian.
>
> Christine Nmanen, 46, Vietnamese
> American, San Jose, Calif.

Contributions are from the New Your Times
Before this rise in hate, it was my parents calling me every other day to check in on me and if I'm doing OK. Now it's me calling them.

Jamie, 28, Korean American, Laurel, Md.

I signed my daughter up for a charter school recently. My husband was filling out the forms and he said we could only choose one ethnicity for my daughter. So he chose white and he didn't choose Asian. I have misgivings about that. But we only had one choice. And I thought, well, she's growing up in the U.S. I guess she is more white now than she is Asian.

Christine Nmanen, 46, Vietnamese American, San Jose, Calif.

I am a single Chinese working mother living with my only daughter in Central Indiana. Before the pandemic, we lived like many other friendly and kind neighbors in my community.

Now, I find myself remaining constantly alert. When I take a walk in my neighborhood, when I stroll down an aisle in the supermarket, whenever there are strangers around me, I am on guard.

I start to feel a little uncomfortable when the conversation turns to accusing the diplomatic relationship with China. I no longer feel free to talk about everything and anything with friends as I used to. I started to alienate myself, after so many years taking my community as an integral part of my life. I began to think I am different and maybe I should leave the table.

But this is still where home is. I will stay, and I hope I can eventually regain the sense of security I used to have.

Jane T., 42, Chinese, Indiana

My parents raised my two older sisters and me with a lot of fear, and I would very openly criticize what I believed to be racist sentiments from them. Fear of other races, fear of hate and violence directed at us, fear of us having mixed-race children one day.

Now that I'm an adult witnessing and experiencing the racial bias and hate in this country, I see what my parents were warning me about from the very beginning. As much as I didn't want it to be true, race very much matters in America.

Geraldine Lim, 33, first generation
Chinese American, Oakland, Calif.

My family is Cambodian and we immigrated to the U.S. when I was just 3 days old — escaping the communist regime called the Khmer Rouge in the late '70s/early '80s. I am immensely lucky that my parents escaped a war torn country and resettled here in America.

I grew up in a western suburb of Chicago that was predominantly white and affluent. From an early age, it was apparent I was different from the other children. We lived in the only Section 8 housing offered in that area. My childhood wasn't exactly happy and easy. I grew up with Latino and African American neighbors that sometimes treated me more racist than Caucasian people I went to school with. I was regularly called derogatory names growing up and was bullied because I was Asian. I remember this very clearly and it has had an impact on me to this day. There were times when I felt really, really lonely growing up as an Asian child.

Now I have a more heightened sense of awareness that I'm Asian and that there may be neighbors, people in the community, at the grocery store or at work who may not like me because they see me as an Asian man and they connect that with the notion that the coronavirus originated from an Asian country — China. I'm not even Chinese and I've never even been to China; I've lived my whole life in America.

I'm a husband, and a father to two cute little women. My wife, Katherine, is Caucasian. We are two working professionals in management positions just trying to raise our family. Working hard and trying to earn a living. And now I have to worry about being randomly, physically attacked because of my skin color. Sad is not the right word. It's disbelief. It's tremendously awful. It's this heightened sense of potential violence toward me that I now have to live with and look out for.

Samuel Kong, 41, Cambodian American, Chicago

I rejected my Korean identity completely when I was young because I was embarrassed and ashamed to be Asian. It wasn't until college that I became interested in the culture. I ended up living in Korea for a few years.

I now make my own kimchi and cook primarily Korean food, listen exclusively to Korean music. I study the Korean language every day. I am so proud now and it's taken a long time to get there.

But the rise in anti-Asian sentiment made me feel ashamed yet again. If I were just white, life would be so much easier. I feel so resentful sometimes of my circumstance. Why couldn't I just have stayed in Korea?

Kim Y., Korean American, New Jersey

I think particularly being an Asian American woman, you find yourself in the position of being vulnerable a lot and being perceived as vulnerable. And even if you consider yourself a very strong person, your perception of vulnerability makes you an easy target for violence because people think they can take advantage of you.

Indu Radhakrishnan, 23, South Asian, Baltimore

At the beginning of the pandemic, as I was going through an airport en route to my flight, I was spit on by a stranger. I was in shock.

But what was more crushing wasn't the saliva dripping down my face. It was looking around and realizing that the dozen people around me simply pretended like it never happened. No one cared or no one wanted to say anything. The silence was complicity in the act of hate. I went from being a "model minority" to being used as spitting target practice.

That moment made me realize that I needed to speak up. I went from trying to fit in and blend in my entire life to asking questions and trying to raise awareness to our communities, even if it meant having tough conversations and pointing out that everyday turns of phrase that some would call funny are what I and many Asian Americans and Pacific Islanders would call belittling and offensive.

Jeff Le, 38, Vietnamese American, Washington, D.C.

I grew up in Alabama and Mississippi, where most people still talk about race as a Black and white issue.

My father, himself the victim of many instances of anti-Asian discrimination, denies systemic racism exists and believes protesting (against what he sees as anecdotal episodes) would bring unwanted consequences, that it's better to remain under the radar even if it means enduring occasional hatred. Ten years ago, I might have agreed with him.

Siew David Hii, 23, Chinese American, Raleigh, N.C.

I was raised in a predominantly white place and for the longest time, I believed I could assimilate myself into whiteness.

I knew other Asian Americans who went to language school and had communities of other Asian Americans. I rejected that as much as I could because I thought I was American first.

As I've become an adult, I realize that it doesn't matter how I think of myself; some others will see me the exact same way as the people who embraced their heritage tighter. It's literally about nothing aside from how we look.

Sam You, 34, Taiwanese American, Los Angeles

As a Pakistani American, I have found it more and more confusing to use the term Asian American to identify myself in recent months.

I was a young child when 9/11 happened, and I remember how scared I was of words like "terrorist" and "Osama" because my family had nailed it into me that using these words would get our whole family into big trouble. I dealt with that anxiety any time another terrorist attack was being covered on the news. I have seen parallels between that and the kind of disgusting anti-Asian sentiment other Asian Americans are feeling now.

While I sometimes see "Asian American" used as an umbrella term for all Asians, a lot of the recent violence and racist sentiments have been directed toward East Asians specifically and not so much toward South Asians. Since I feel that most South Asians look so physically distinct from other Asians, and since recent hate crimes seem to target people based on identifying East Asian physical characteristics, I have been conflicted about whether or not I even feel targeted by any of this. I have simultaneously felt the need to speak up about racist anti-Asian sentiment I have felt in the past while also wanting to step back and let East Asian Americans discuss how this is all affecting them.

Waleed Khan, 23, Chicago

Being Asian means wondering if someone is going to say your name right continuing to wonder if things are about race or not. starting to cleanse away my self-hate and shame and learning that white supremacy is the enemy, not myself. Resisting the model minority and creating our own narratives and stories. being proud of your name, whatever it is. Finding peace in the past and building a different future. Knowing we don't need to be white or white-adjacent in order to be human, unlike what the media has taught us. Who we are is human enough.

Yue Xiang, 27, Chinese American, Philadelphia

I don't really know who I am, or what I am, but I'm starting to embrace whatever it means to be Asian American, although I'll tell you the truth: When I moved from Florida to California, I wasn't Asian enough for the Asians, and to the Americans I'm never American enough.

Karen Ong, 37, Chinese American, Galveston, Texas

I've learned over time that Asian American voices shouldn't be heard only when we are feeling like our lives are being threatened. We should be vocal long before and long after the news cameras turn away from us to focus on the next big headline.

Michael Thai, 38, Vietnamese American, San Diego

Despite the fact that my mother's family has resided in this country for four generations, we are perpetually viewed as foreigners, making assimilation seem impossible. That is the reason that I personally find the "American" in "Asian American" to be so important, because I am, culturally, by birth and in every other way, 100 percent American.

> Amy Tieh-mei Chang, 46, Chinese
> American, Alameda, Calif.

I have always viewed our status in this country as being one of second-class citizens. While, in the past, American-born people of Asian descent have said that they were grateful for their parents or ancestors having come to this country to give them a better life, I have long felt that this was a wrong decision on the part of my parents.

Seeking economic gain and being misguided by this country's false promises of equality, they came here and now I and my descendants are basically stuck being second-class citizens in a country that we can never truly call our own because it seems to disown us. I also find it hard to feel any patriotism or even loyalty to this country as it is hard to love something that seems to hate you back.

> Eugene, New York City

I'd like to say that we're not a monolith. Just because the virus started in China doesn't mean that we're all Chinese. There are many other countries in Asia. And just because we're Asian doesn't mean that we're loyal to other governments and that we're trying to play against you and that we're on another team. On the contrary, we're on the same team. We're Americans. We see ourselves as Americans, and we hope that you do, too.

> Elie Mala, 29, Thai American, New York City

When do we stay and fight for an equal and just piece of the American pie, and when do we choose a better life elsewhere, like our parents and grandparents did?

Our ancestors were pragmatic — they wanted to provide a better life for themselves and their children, and they did everything they could to make that happen, even if it meant leaving their homes and venturing into unfamiliar lands where they didn't speak the language.

What if that better life is no longer in the U.S.? What if that better life is actually possible in many other places now, including the very lands our ancestors came from?

Jane W. Wang, Taiwanese American, Taipei, Taiwan

Asian American has become a term that is co-opted by states, corporations and other oppressive forces and no longer stands for the radical solidarity it once did. Sure, coalition building is useful — but I am interested in a coalition that doesn't erase the oppression that occurs within and among "Asian" communities. As a Sikh American, I don't want to be labeled as Asian American because other "Asian" communities express discriminatory anti-Sikh prejudice. I don't want to have the same name as my oppressors.

Asian American no longer captures the nuances and layered oppressions faced by marginalized "Asian" communities, such as Hmong, Cambodian, Laotian, Dalit, Sri Lankan, Assamese, Sikh, Indian Muslim, Indian Christian and Uyghur communities, among others. I want to be seen. I want to define myself. I don't want to be defined by a generic label that has lost its power of resistance.

Kanwalroop Kaur Singh, 29, Sikh
American, San Jose, Calif.

I was adopted from China into a white family, and the rise in hate crimes and violence and racist rhetoric has brought up some difficult conversations with my parents.

My parents see me as their daughter, someone they love and are proud of. They don't see me through the eyes of society: a young Asian woman who is often hit on for being exotic, or constantly asked where I am from. It's hard to have these conversations with my white family, to get them to understand and to recognize that even as they try, they will never fully understand my experience.

Like most white people who are currently trying to understand what it means to be a person of color in America, their intentions are good but the burden to educate is on me.

Annie LaFleur, 25, Chinese, Portland, Ore.

Like many second-generation Asian Americans, I was the child with the stinky lunch and the only one among friends whose parents had an accent. It was embarrassing. Now, what's embarrassing is that I ever felt that shame about my family's roots.

Jenny Wu Donahue, 33, Chinese American, New York City

As an American of Chinese descent, I feel like we are being given two options, neither of which truly solve our problem. The first comes from the older generation, those who tell us that our silence will be our survival. Then there's the second option, from those my age, who feel like we have to show more than just our passports and polished American English as proof of our belonging. We aren't even unified in our beliefs, and that's our greatest weakness.

Chase, 24, Chinese American, New York City

My grandparents were interned during World War II. This had a profound impact on my family financially and emotionally. Due to the anti-Japanese postwar sentiment, my parents were encouraged to assimilate as much as possible into the dominant (white) culture. Growing up in the 1980s, I experienced some discrimination, yet it wasn't until the last decade that I became more educated and engaged as an advocate for racial equity, including standing with my Black and brown friends to fight injustice.

Elaine Ikeda, 56, Japanese American,
Redwood City, Calif.

I only think of myself as Asian American when I check off an identity box on a form. Otherwise, I'm a Sikh American, a Punjabi American and a South Asian American. The Asian community is not a monolith, and the term "Asian" to describe all of our various experiences and cultures is not helpful or accurate.

Jo Kaur, 38, Sikh American, Queens, N.Y.

I'm married to a Caucasian man and we used to think it's possible for us to belong. Now we don't. Now people look at me differently when I'm alone versus when I'm with him. I don't feel as safe. I carry a passport that says "U.S. citizen" to prove to people that I belong. Though at times I wonder if it's a reminder to myself that I do.

Anh W., 42, Vietnamese American,
Eden Prairie, Minn.

Like all immigrants, I have an American dream. As a queer woman from a country marred by military dictatorships, censorships and blood coups, I saw the United States as a safe haven where diversity is celebrated.

That sense of security and optimism was shattered after my assault. It took me a month after my assault before I could confess to my father, who dreamed of being reunited with me after my medical training. A former monk known for his calm and gentle presence, my father cried for the first time in my life. He asked, "Are you hurt?" I hope to one day be able to tell him, "Yes, I was hurt, but I am also healing."

Oranicha Jumreornvong, 26, Thai, New York City

Biculturalism is an important part of the immigrant experience. It allows immigrants to keep some of their cultural identity and make it a part of the host country's culture. This helps them feel connected and welcomed in the new place they call home. It also gives new perspectives on issues that can arise from different ways of thinking, as well as opportunities for dialogue and understanding between different cultures.

However, sometimes a host country may have specific guidelines or restrictions on what types of cultural practices are acceptable, which can make biculturalism difficult to achieve. For example, a country may welcome certain foods brought by an immigrant group but not accept their religious practices. This kind of piecemeal acceptance makes it hard for people to fully retain their cultural identity while still being welcomed in the host country.

In recent years, globalization has connected societies and cultures in a way that has never been seen before. As a result, countries around the world are becoming increasingly multicultural, with people migrating from one place to another for various reasons. This cultural diversity can bring about many positive changes to a country's social and economic landscape but it can also create challenges when it comes to fostering acceptance and understanding between different groups.

In order to ensure that all citizens feel welcome regardless of their background or culture, countries must strive to maintain immigrants' sense of belonging by properly recognizing and accepting biculturalism - or the conscious effort to maintain one's cultural identity while also embracing other cultures. Policymakers should aim to create laws and policies that accommodate different cultures without diminishing anyone's sense of belonging.

In addition, citizens should be encouraged to learn about other cultures in order to should design laws that are flexible enough to accommodate different cultures without diminishing anyone's sense of belonging. Furthermore, citizens should be encouraged to learn about and appreciate different cultures in order to foster greater understanding and acceptance between different groups.

Biculturalism can not only help bring people together but it can also help combat discrimination based on culture or identity. It provides immigrants with the opportunity to express their cultural differences openly while still feeling connected to their new country. Additionally, it allows for increased communication between members of different communities which is key in creating an environment of inclusivity and mutual respect.

In order for biculturalism to truly take root, countries must ensure that they are offering a platform where all voices can be heard regardless of background or culture. Additionally, education is key to creating a more inclusive society where individuals from all walks of life can coexist. Educating citizens on the value of cultural diversity can encourage people to be more open-minded and accepting of others.

Ultimately, biculturalism is essential in order for countries to foster greater understanding and acceptance between different cultures. Through proper recognition and understanding of different cultures, policymakers can create laws that accommodate different backgrounds while encouraging citizens to learn about other cultures in order to promote mutual respect and appreciation. Biculturalism is an important part of globalization and should not be overlooked

14

Education & Policy

Making a Positive Impact Education
is the most powerful weapon
which you can use to change the world.
—Nelson Mandela

As the workforce demographics continue to diversify, becoming an increasingly heterogeneous environment, businesses have begun to focus on acknowledging and celebrating the differences represented by their employees in hopes of encouraging a more productive culture. Businesses that facilitate a diverse culture, in which all members are treated equally and have access to opportunities, have proven to grow stronger financially, socially, and ethically, as we have previously discussed.

But introducing diversity initiatives into an organization is often a challenge for employees and management. A culture of diversity tends to challenge current values and worldviews, sometimes initiating conflict that makes current employees feel uncomfortable and threatened.

If we want to achieve diversity in the workplace, we need to approach it strategically. The way the company introduces its diversity initiative is just as important as the program itself. Whether or not a company is successful with its program depends on whether or not it anticipates and addresses how people will feel when they are faced with big changes at their job.

In addition to communicating realistic expectations, companies should take steps to ensure members of minority groups understand the goal and scope of new policies.

The most effective means of communicating your new racial and ethnic diversity policy to employees is by combining email, internal media networks, including social media, posters, and mailing in a consistent manner. By having messaging that can accommodate the different languages and literacy levels of employees, you can be ensured that everyone understands the new policies.

In addition to this, companies should create an effective but confidential mechanism for workers to air their concerns that allows workers to file grievances without fear of reprisal or retribution.

If your organization has a policy prohibiting discrimination and harassment, and you enforce that policy, you should not have to deal with diversity complaints; however, even in the best of organizations, you might still be faced with such a complaint. If so, it is vital that you have clear processes for reporting, investigating, and resolving such complaints. Doing so will make it easier for employees who feel like they have been unfairly treated to come forward and will minimize the impact of any complaints that do arise.

This is why written policies and procedures are necessary for effective diversity and inclusion management.

In addition to having an internal grievance policy in place, you'll want to put together a complaint procedure manual (CP) that outlines the steps you'll take when dealing with complaints. This is also useful if you have employees who work elsewhere but have a connection to your organization. If they are aware there is a process in place for handling complaints, they're more likely to come forward if they feel uncertain about what steps to take or what their rights are.

It is critical to have a step-by-step process for employees to follow when filing diversity complaints. This process should take them through the steps of reporting and resolving complaints. The process should be easy to find, intelligible to all, and clearly laid out. It should be included in training and regularly communicated to employees.

So what should be included in your complaint procedure manual (CP)?

1. Who's responsible for dealing with the complaint? This is usually going to list a person or department (or someone else) who will be involved in resolving the issue.
2. A detailed timeline of events showing how the violation occurred, with dates and times that support your claims.
3. The due date for filing a report.
4. The specific documentation required or recommended. 5. The steps that will be taken in investigating a complaint.
5. The time frame in which the investigation will be completed.
6. What steps will be taken if the complaint is found to be without merit?
7. What steps will be taken if the complaint is found to be valid?

When an employee grievance or complaint process has been created, it should be published for all employees to review at any time. Employers must also ensure that a diversity complaint procedure is available in a format readable by employees with disabilities. This helps ensure that all employees will know how to file a complaint and how to handle one if they need to.

As part of diversity, equity, and inclusion training, you might choose to focus on a specific area, such as gender or race. Alternatively, you can do a broader diversity, equity, and inclusion training around a variety of issues in order to provide your employees with more information.

When creating a training program that aims to fight workplace bias, you must present the material in a way that helps employees to better understand the issues. By using stories to get participants thinking and interacting with each other, you create a training experience in which people learn from one another. When structured properly, training can be effective in changing behavior and helping employees understand the importance of valuing differences and creating a workplace of equity.

Organizations should avoid promoting shame or guilt as much as possible with their diversity, equity, and inclusion training.

To motivate trainees, show them how the training will give them increased self-insight and understanding. Tie the material to their personal experiences and allow them to share their own stories as they go along. Again, to maximize the benefits of training, you must engage your participants. For example, have them work in small groups to discuss key concepts and have them role-play certain scenarios. If the participants are disengaged in the training, they will not benefit from it.

When creating diversity, equity, and inclusion training for your company, you can adopt a model based on what works in your workplace or you can hire an outside company. You can create diversity training programs that are tailored to your specific needs. The process of planning such a program consists of observing the company's policies, current situations, and the expressed needs of your employees.

Method(s) of Delivery

The goal of any training program, whether it's diversity training or otherwise, is to increase individual and organizational performance. It is also important that your organization does not rely solely on one method of delivering a diversity training program. Trainees need opportunities to learn through observation, experience, individual reflection, and group interaction.

The support of senior management is also crucial in any corporate change initiative, especially one as critical as diversity training. Senior management should be visible in their support of the program, including attendance at all seminars and/or workshops.

The following are some of the methods you can use to deliver a successful diversity training program:

- Individual training: This program comprises self-paced learning materials and computer-assisted learning. The trainees learn at their own pace and time. This is a good method to use when the trainee has little time to go for classroom training. The advantage of this method is that the trainee can take control of his or her learning process.

- Organizational in-house training: Here the organization hires a consultant or trainer to train its employees. The advantage of this method is that the trainer can customize the content according to an organization's needs as well as its culture.

- External seminar or workshop training: This approach is suitable for organizations with no internal resources or expertise in diversity management. Here employees attend training sessions organized by different organizations or institutions outside their workplace and environments. The advantage is that it gives employees an opportunity to network with people from other companies and even get inspired by them.

- Blended learning: Blended learning combines web-based instruction with some in-person sessions as well as other types of activities, such as self-assessments and simulations. This model can provide the advantages of both methods without their disadvantages—in other words, it can be fast and inexpensive while still being engaging and effective.

- Web-based training: Online training is generally faster to create than in-person programs because it's easier to scale the content. It's also less expensive because there are no travel costs or time away from work; however, it can produce less of an impact on employees because they're not getting the human interaction that comes with a live facilitator.

In these times of increasing social tension, it is important to assess the effectiveness of your diversity, equity, and inclusion training program.

You'll want to know if employees are responding positively to your training and if it is helping them become more aware of issues surrounding diversity, equity, and inclusion in the workplace.

It is also important that your organization does not rely solely on one method of delivering a diversity training program. Most diversity training programs fail because they are too narrow in scope, too superficial, and/ or too theoretical.

The best tactic for delivering a diversity training program is to use an experiential model that encourages the participants to learn through doing, as we have touched on. It is very important to develop a comprehensive program that addresses all four levels of diversity learning: awareness, knowledge, skill, and application.

The first level, awareness, focuses on helping people recognize their biases and stereotypes to see how this shape their perceptions of other people. A good way to achieve this is to have participants complete an inventory of their own cultural experiences, as well as those of others they have known or worked with in the past.

The second level, knowledge, involves understanding the different types of diversity, including those based on race and ethnicity, gender, sexual orientation, and mental or physical ability, as well as the barriers these groups have faced throughout history and continue to face today.

Skill building involves learning specific strategies for interacting more effectively with different people at work. One strategy used in communication skill–building programs is to teach people how to identify differences in communication style—for example, between men and women—and learn how to adapt accordingly when conversing with people from other groups. Application means giving people the tools they need to make meaningful change after the training ends. After becoming more aware of their own biases, building their knowledge base about diversity issues, and developing their skills around inclusive communication, people are motivated to seek out opportunities to use those tools in real-life work situations.

It is important to assess the effectiveness of your diversity, equity, and inclusion training program. You can use the following six questions to think about the appropriateness of your training for your organization:

1. Does the training address the needs of all employees?
2. Does each participant receive an equal opportunity to participate in the training?

3. Is there a sufficient level of awareness about how to best implement the program at your company?
4. Do you have a clear understanding of what each employee should do and not do when they move forward with implementing their new skills?
5. Did you evaluate any potential liability, such as discrimination claims or harassment claims?
6. Did you implement a post-training evaluation that allows employees to provide feedback on the program content and facilitator performance?

Adding to this, you can hold focus groups with small groups of employees to gather feedback about what they like or don't like about the training or periodically distribute surveys to all employees to find out how they're responding to the training and how it's helping them do their jobs better.

Diversity training may be mandatory, but in many cases it's not enough for someone to merely check the box and say they've taken the class. The goal is not just to have people take a class on diversity but actually learn something from it.

Understanding how to interact with people who aren't like you is especially important in a professional setting, where working as a team is crucial for an organization's success.

Although diversity education can be controversial because it may involve teaching or discussing sensitive issues about race, religion, sexuality, political views, and the like, and while it might seem daunting to try to educate your employees about every one of these diverse groups, it's important that you do so.

Diversity education is important for everyone and should be taken seriously. The problems with diversity are bigger than the thing that we see—racism. There are many unspoken issues and constructs we don't know about, but it doesn't mean there shouldn't be any attempt to change our views for the better. In short, diversity education is providing opportunities to challenge harmful beliefs and attitudes. These biases may not always be explicit or intentional, but they're still harmful.

Education has the power to help people recognize their own biases and move beyond them to create a more positive environment for everyone.

A workplace is a place of opportunity, but that potential is squandered when that place is not an arena for each person's unique talents. The workplace should be the widest possible avenue for human potential to find its highest expression. We fulfill our potential and enhance everyone's opportunity for personal growth when we create workplaces where diversity education and diversity training are present before new hires begin their careers and continue an ongoing basis throughout all levels of an organization.

If we want our workplaces to be diverse, we need to teach people to value diversity from the beginning. We need the values and mindsets of diversity, multiculturalism, and tolerance to be part of the education process.

In the United States, measuring diversity and inclusion successes is particularly important because it affects economic growth. If a nation cannot tap into its talent pool in a way that creates opportunities for people of all different backgrounds and identities, the nation will be less competitive in the global economy. Many factors contribute to this problem, but we can take action right now to close the gaps by making diversity education a key part of the education process.

15

Where Are We Now?

Diversity has become a focal point for debate and discussion both inside and outside the workplace. The reason that workplace diversity has become such a hot topic among businesses is that it is thought to be one of the biggest keys to success in today's business world. It is also the topic that has brought us here, to this final chapter.

If you are a diversity, equity, and inclusion professional or hold an HR role, you might be tempted to point to your organization's diversity training program as a solution. While training is a necessary component of any DEI strategy, it is not enough. What is needed instead is accountability at every level in the workplace. Accountability helps to create a strong foundation for diversity and inclusion. When employees see leaders who are held accountable for their words and actions, they will feel more comfortable speaking up if they ever experience discrimination.

Accountability applies to everyone—from CEOs who set the tone of the organization to HR professionals who establish policies and procedures to middle managers who create a culture of respect and dignity to individuals at all levels who speak up when they see or hear disrespectful behavior. Accountability also creates a culture in which employees feel ownership over their organization's success and a responsibility to help fix its problems.

Diversity and inclusion are critical for companies to achieve and sustain a competitive advantage. Although big strides have been made in DEI, there is still a long way to go; it is not enough. The United States has changed dramatically in the last five years. We're at a pivotal moment in our country's history as we grapple with issues of inequity, division, and discrimination. Now more than ever, it's clear how important it is to have a long-term vision for what kind of society we want to be and to take powerful steps in that direction.

For many Americans, the reality of these issues is something they can choose to ignore. This is because change is often resisted by people who are comfortable with the status quo. Employees who have been at a company for many years may not understand the reasons why certain changes in policy or hiring practices are being made, such as an increase in recruiting diverse candidates.

This resistance can take many forms, from employees refusing to work with those who are different to managers actively ignoring recruiting practices. There is a myriad of reasons as to why there may be resistance to workplace diversity, but the fact of the matter is that change is needed. Progress doesn't require people to think outside their comfort zone. It just requires them to accept different viewpoints and other ways of doing things. Understandably, change may cause anxiety, but in order to advance we have to have the ability and willingness to accept change. This seems like a small price to pay.

Change is hard to accept when you are accustomed to the way things are. This can manifest itself in a variety of ways, from a simple unwillingness to learn something new to hostility toward the new people and changes being made. The unwillingness to learn and the resistance to change are two of the biggest threats to our well-being. But these issues are not just workplace issues; they are societal ones.

A society that is unwilling to change is a society that has not accepted one of the most important lessons history has taught us: everything changes. The sooner we realize how pervasive this truth is, the better we can prepare ourselves for it. The way we do business has changed dramatically, for one thing. Our lives are changing at an ever-faster pace. We see it in the way we communicate, travel, and work; how we learn; and what we eat, buy, and wear.

History has also taught us that no matter how stable society may appear, everything is always subject to change—often in ways we never expect. The fall of the Roman Empire was unthinkable at its height; most Romans genuinely believed their civilization would endure forever. Yet it fell victim to political instability and foreign invasion in just a few centuries' time. In science, technology, culture, and politics, we're able to adapt quicker than ever before. We're also able to share information on a global scale with unprecedented ease. We can reach out and connect with people all around the world, regardless of political or cultural differences. The racial reckoning that defined 2019 has led to more conversations about diversity, even in the workplace. We saw more people than ever before, from all walks of life, race, religion, and gender, joining together to fight for racial equality. We saw more companies than ever before taking an active stand against racism. And we saw consumers paying more attention to the brands they support, expecting them to take a stand on social issues as well.

In 2019 companies finally sat up and listened. The pandemic forced many businesses to adopt a more flexible work-from-home policy, which led to employees wanting more flexibility in other areas too. Companies were forced to look at their policies and how they affected their people.

This was great news for Black employees, who have asked for years for more diversity, equity, inclusion, and belonging. But we must be cautious. Companies must not fall into the trap of "woke washing," where they only make changes on the surface. True change comes from inclusion at all levels and concrete actions that will benefit those who are underrepresented in the workplace, including Black people and other people of color.

As we look back on the past few years, it's clear that most companies did not make good on their promises. Yes, there's been an increase in companies committing to diversity, equity, and inclusion initiatives. But we have yet to see tangible actions being taken. Many companies are stuck in an endless cycle of diversity hiring without addressing the issue of retention. Companies are not retaining the diverse individuals they bring into their organizations. If a company hires ten Black people, but only two remain after three years, that's a clear sign there's a problem.

According to a new report from the Center for Talent Innovation, 62 percent of women and 47 percent of minorities are leaving their employers by the midlevel point in their careers. This results in a huge loss of productivity and talent. Companies are spending nearly $8 billion per year on diversity training and development. But this investment isn't paying off. In fact, companies are not retaining the diverse individuals they bring into their organizations. The average cost of losing an employee to turnover is 21 percent of their annual salary. This means that the financial burden for losing these employees can be significant.

One of the reasons for this is that companies have historically overlooked the importance of retaining employees and instead focused on hiring or developing talent. While finding new people is important, it's also important to take care of the ones you already have.

When diverse employees see their colleagues depart, it sends a message about who can succeed and be happy at an organization. The result is less diverse teams and an even greater challenge for companies looking to hire from underrepresented groups.

A Forbes Insights survey shows that more than half (53 percent) of workers want to make a change, with 25 percent saying they plan on leaving their current job within the next six months. With so many people looking for new jobs, it's critical for companies to take a long, hard look at their retention strategies and consider how they can retain the diverse talent that makes up their workforce. While the pandemic has brought about new challenges for employers, it also presents an opportunity for companies to attract and retain diverse talent. So why aren't more companies focusing on retention? It could be because they simply don't know how to do it.

A recent survey by the Society for Human Resource Management of more than 500 human resource professionals found that 40 percent believe their organizations are "ineffective" at retaining employees. The process of improving minority retention starts with education. If you're a company leader or in HR, start by examining your current practices. If you don't already have an inclusion and diversity policy in place, now is the time to develop one. You'll also want to ensure that all hiring managers are aware of the policy and can clearly articulate it to candidates during the interview process.

It's important to identify any potential areas—whether that's pay equity, lack of upward mobility, or implicit bias—where your company may not be providing equal opportunities for minorities so you can develop strategies to address those issues specifically. Then make sure those strategies are part of your overall retention program.

In fact, most of the solutions are obvious—pay your people what they're worth, give them more control over their schedules, and make sure they're happy with the work they do—but others are less intuitive.

For instance, did you know that allowing employees to work remotely can reduce turnover by about 50 percent? Or that giving employees specific, actionable feedback can increase their performance by up to 44 percent? It's not just about paying your people well and giving them good benefits. It's about making them feel like valued members of your company and offering them opportunities for professional growth.

Recruiting and hiring are only two steps in the overall employee life cycle. In order to retain these employees and cultivate them into future leaders, companies need to focus on employee engagement and communication. Diversity drives innovation. It's a simple concept—the more perspectives you have in a room, the more ideas will be generated.

Gone are the days of turning a blind eye toward diversity. Companies are realizing that their bottom line is directly connected to the level of diversity they have representing their company. While all of this is important, nothing can be achieved unless there is respect. One of the major components of racism or harassment is a lack of respect for the other party.

Managing respect is a crucial element of success in any company. Respect and trust are the two most important elements in workplace relationships. Trust is a crucial element of success in any company. There's a direct relationship between team members being able to trust each other and being accountable to each other. When employees are accountable

to each other, they're more likely to complete projects on time, work together effectively on larger projects, and go out of their way to help one another when necessary. All these factors can improve productivity and performance at work, which leads to career advancement opportunities for your team members and increased profits for the company overall.

Many people have been in situations in which they're working with a team, and there is a distinct lack of respect for each other or for an organization or client. It's easy to get frustrated when you feel like this because it's impossible to bring your best effort to any project if you don't have the support of those around you. In a professional setting, it's easy to lose track of the fact that the people you work with are just that: people. As a result, human elements like empathy and respect can get left behind. Each year the business world spends billions of dollars on diversity initiatives and training. Yet every day there are more headlines about the challenges of workforce diversity.

Everyone wants the same things from employment. They want a fair shot at advancing in their field. They want to be compensated fairly for their work. They want to be able to balance work with the rest of their lives. And they want their workplace to feel like somewhere that values them as an individual, not just as a pawn in the greater scheme of corporate profits. Diversity is key in achieving those goals.

In the United States, workplace diversity has evolved over the past few decades but still has much further to go. The age of minorities, women, and older workers has increased steadily over the past twenty-five years, while the share of white men has fallen. The change has been driven by several factors, including an influx of immigrants and a growing population of women in the workforce. While workplaces are becoming more diverse, they still have a long way to go before being considered representative of the country's overall demographics, and that's especially true when it comes to leadership positions.

There is a lot of positive change in regards to diversity that is taking place in the workforce, but the numbers are nowhere near where they should be for a country as diverse as ours. That leaves a lot of work to be done. There is no question that women and minorities in the United States face systemic indignities and unfair obstacles in life, at school, at work, and in all other

aspects of society. Not only is diversity an essential part of a healthy society, but it's also essential for a healthy economy.

Workplace diversity for the outside appears well entrenched in corporate America. Despite an entire industry devoted to applying diversity principles to change corporate culture, diversity remains an ambiguous and misunderstood concept to most that can clearly benefit from continued frank and thoughtful dialogue.

In 1963 at height of the civil rights movement, Martin Luther King Jr spoke the famous words "I have a dream that one day this nation will rise up and live out the true meaning of its creed: We hold these truths to be self-evident, that all men are created equal." from the steps of the Lincoln Memorial in Washington, D.C. He was not the first to raise his voice from those steps with a message of hope for America's future. That distinction belongs to the world-famous contralto Marian Anderson, whose performance at the Lincoln Memorial on April 9, 1939, made a compelling case for the transformative power of music and in a place typically associated with the power of words.

Anderson was an international superstar in the 1930s—a singer described as "a voice such as one hears once in a hundred years." But if race had been no impediment to her career abroad, there were still places in the United States where a Black woman was simply not welcome, no matter how famous. What surprised Anderson and many other Americans was to discover in 1939 that one such place was a venue called Constitution Hall, owned and operated by the Daughters of the American Revolution in the capital of a nation "dedicated to the proposition that all men are created equal." When the D.A.R. refused to allow, Anderson to perform at Constitution Hall because of her skin color.

The invitation to perform on the steps of the Lincoln Memorial came directly from the Secretary of the Interior, Harold L. Ickes, who proclaimed in his introduction of Marian Anderson on that Easter Sunday that "Genius draws no color line." There was nothing overtly political in the selection of songs Anderson performed that day before a gathered crowd of 75,000 and a live radio audience of millions. But the message inherent in an African American woman singing "My Country' Tis of Thee" while standing before the shrine of America's Great Emancipator was crystal clear.

"Genius draws no color lines."

-Harold Ickes

In 2021 Harvard Business Review reported that 16 employees in 14 countries had been surveyed approximately range and inclusion inside the place of job, and the findings had been telling. The Review states that "1/2 of all numerous personnel said that they see bias as part of their everyday paintings experience. ... with the aid of comparison, white heterosexual adult males, who tend to dominate the management ranks, have been 13 percent factors more likely to say that the everyday revel in and foremost choices are freed from bias."

How can we begin to solve this problem and foster a more inclusive society? We must all recognize we have unconscious biases, and we must be able to confront them inside ourselves. We've come a long way but still have a longer way to go.

Where there's life, there's hope."

— Stephen Hawking

Property of White River Valley Museum, Auburn

230

Acknowledgments

A very special thank-you to the following women for their support, honesty, and bravery in sharing their own personal stories and keeping me motivated to finish this book: Monique Boyd Loni Mendez Janaiah C. von Hassel anonymous contributors

Resource

Vaughn, B. E. (2002). A heuristic model of managing emotions in race relations training. In E. Davis-Russell (Ed.), Multicultural Education, Research, Intervention, & Training (pp. 296-318). San Francisco, CA.: Jossey-Bass.

Day, H. R. (1983). Race relations training in the military. In D. Landis & R. Brislin (Eds.), Handbook of Intercultural Training, Vol. II: Issues in training methodology (pp. 241-289). New York: Pergamon Press.

Devine, P. G., & Monteith, M. J. (1993). The role of discrepancy associated affect in prejudice reduction. In D. Mackie & D. Hamiltonâ (Eds.), Affect, cognition, and stereotyping: Interactive processes in group perception (pp.137-166), San Diego, CA.: Harcourt, Brace, & Jananovich.

"HISTORY OF DIVERSITY TRAINING & ITS PIONEERS." Diversity Officer Magazine, diversityofficermagazine.com/diversity-inclusion/the-history-of-diversity-training-its-pioneers/ [iii] "Alain Dehaze Quotes." Brainyquote, Xplore

McCormick, Kate. "The evolution of workplace diversity." Hous. Law (2007): 10.

Allison, M., and Smith, S. (1990). "Leisure and quality of life: Issues facing racial and ethnic minority elderly." Therapeutic Recreation Journal, 24 (3), 50–6.

McCormick, Kate, 2007. "The evolution of workplace diversity." Houston Law Review.

Ran Abramitzky, Leah Platt Boustan, and Katherine Eriksson. (2014). "A Nation of Immigrants: Assimilation and Economic Outcomes in the Age of Mass Migration." Journal of Political Economy. 122(3): 467-506.

Ran Abramitzky, Leah Platt Boustan, and Katherine Eriksson. (2016). "Cultural Assimilation During the Age of Mass Migration." Working paper, and references therein.

Ran Abramitzky, and Leah Platt Boustan. (2016a). "Immigration in American Economic History." NBER Working Paper No. 21882, and references therein.

Vasiliki Fouka. (2015). "Backlash: The Unintended Effects of Language Prohibition in U.S. Schools after World War I." Manuscript.

American Psychiatric Association, The Diagnostic and Statistical Manual of Mental Disorders 5th Edition (Arlington, VA: American Psychiatric Press, 2013).

"About ASAN," Autistic Self Advocacy Network, accessed Autism Speaks Return of Organization Exempt From Income Tax, 2010, Form 990 OMB 1545-0047.

"Facts and Statistics," Autism Society, Accessed August 26, 2021

"Data and Statistics," Centers for Disease Control and Prevention—Attention-Deficit Hyperactivity Disorder (ADHD), last modified February 2017, https://www.cdc.gov/ncbddd/adhd/data.html.

"Charles Addams—Quotes," Goodreads, https://www.goodreads.com/quotes/707032-normal-is-an-illusion-what-is-normal-for-the-spider. Acesses.

"Library of the History of Autism Research, Behaviourism and Psychiatry," Neurodiversity.com, Accessed March 1, 2021.

"After you hit a child, you can't just get up and leave him; you are hooked to that child' O. Ivar Lovaas Interview with Paul Chance," Neurodiversity.com

Robin Shulman, "Child Study Center Cancels Autism Ads." Washington Post, December 20, 2007, http://www.washingtonpost.com/wp-dyn/content/article/2007/12/19/AR2007121902230.html.

"About Wrong Planet," Wrong Planet, http://wrongplanet.net/about-wrong-planet/.

Vaughn, B. E. (2002). A heuristic model of managing emotions in race relations training. In E. Davis-Russell (Ed.), Multicultural Education, Research, Intervention, & Training (pp. 296-318). San Francisco, CA.: Jossey-Bass.

Day, H. R. (1983). Race relations training in the military. In D. Landis & R. Brislin (Eds.), Handbook of Intercultural Training, Vol. II: Issues in training methodology (pp. 241-289).

Devine, P. G., & Monteith, M. J. (1993). The role of discrepancy associated affect in prejudice reduction. In D. Mackie & D. Hamiltonâ (Eds.), Affect, cognition, andstereotyping: Interactive processes in group perception (pp.137-166), San Diego, CA.

Harcourt, Brace, & Jananovich. "HISTORY OF DIVERSITY TRAINING & ITS PIONEERS." Diversity Officer Magazine, diversityofficermagazine.com/diversity-inclusion/the-history-of-diversity-training-its-pioneers/ [iii] "Alain Dehaze Quotes." Brainyquote, Xplore

McCormick, Kate, 2007 "The evolution of workplace diversity." Hous. Law, Social Sciences and Education Research Review, Department of Communication, Journalism and Education Sciences, University of Craiova, vol. 3(2), pages 143-149

Aurelia DUMITRU & Andrei Bogdan BUDICÄ,2017. "Informational Content Of The Periodic Synthesis Reports," Annals of the University of Craiova for Journalism, Communication and Management, Department of Communication, Journalism and Education Sciences, University of Craiova, vol. 3(1), pages 49-61, August.

Bianca Teodorescu, 2017. "The communication between the media and tradition," Social Sciences and Education Research Review, Department of Communication, Journalism and Education Sciences, University of Craiova, vol. 4(2), pages 215-221, December.

Sofia Sprechmann, 2020, Secretary-General, Care International

The Global Gender Gap Report 2022, 2022 World Economic Forum

McDonald, L., 2017. Mary Seacole V Florence Nightingale - Nursing Matters. Nursing Matters. http://nursing-matters.com/mary-seacole-v-florence-nightingale-2/>

Seacole, Mary, Wonderful Adventures of Mrs. Seacole in Many Lands

The Department of Labor's Policy & Procedures for Preventing & Eliminating Harassing Conduct in the Workplace (Harassing Conduct Policy) is contained in DLMS 4—chapter 700.

Faragher v. City of Boca Raton, 524 U.S. 775, 788 (1998).

Bertrand, M, Mullainathan, S. "Are Emily And Greg More Employable Than Lakisha And Jamal? A Field Experiment On Labor Market Discrimination." American Economic Review, 2004, v94(4, Sep), 991–1013.

Biernat M., Manis M. "Shifting standards and stereotype-based judgments." Journal of Personality and Social Psychology. 1994 Jan;66(1):5–20.

Burgess D., van Ryn M., Dovidio J., Saha S. "Reducing racial bias among health care providers: lessons from social-cognitive psychology." Journal of General Internal Medicine. 2007 Jun;22(6):882–7.

Carnes M., Devine P. G., Isaac C., Manwell L. B., Ford C. E., Byars-Winston A., Fine E., Sheridan J. T. "Promoting Institutional Change Through Bias Literacy." Journal of Diversity in Higher Education. 2012 Jun;5(2):63–77.

Cooper L. A., Roter D. L., Carson K. A., Beach M. C., Sabin J. A., Greenwald A. G., Inui T. S. "The associations of clinicians' implicit attitudes about race with medical visit communication and patient ratings of interpersonal care." American Journal of Public Health. 2012 May;102(5):979–87.

Dasgupta, N. (2004). "Implicit Ingroup Favoritism, Outgroup Favoritism, and Their Behavioral Manifestations." Social Justice Research, 17(2), 143–169.

Dasgupta, N. (2013). "Implicit Attitudes and Beliefs Adapt to Situations: A Decade of Research on the Malleability of Implicit Prejudice, Stereotypes, and the Self-Concept." Advances in Experimental Social Psychology, 47, 233–279.

Dasgupta, N, Greenwald, A. G. (2001). "On the Malleability of Automatic Attitudes: Combating Automatic Prejudice With Images of Admired and Disliked Individuals." Journal of Personality and Social Psychology, 81(5), 800–814.

Dore, R. A., Hoffman, K. M., Lillard, A. S. and Trawalter, S. (2014). "Children's racial bias in perceptions of others' pain." British Journal of Developmental Psychology, 32: 218–231.

Fiske, S. T. and Taylor, S. E (1991). Social Cognition—International Edition. McGraw-Hill Series in Social Psychology.

Glicksman, Eve. "Unconscious Bias in Academic Medicine: Overcoming the Prejudices We Don't Know We Have." Association of American Medical Colleges. 2016 January.

Green A. R., Carney D. R., Pallin D. J., Ngo L. H., Raymond K. L., Iezzoni L. I., Banaji M. R. "Implicit bias among physicians and its prediction of thrombolysis decisions for black and white patients." Journal of General Internal Medicine. 2007 Sep;22(9):1231–8.

Heilman M. E., Alcott V. B. "What I think you think of me: women's reactions to being viewed as beneficiaries of preferential selection." Journal of Applied Psychology. 2001 Aug;86(4):574–82.

Heilman M. E., Haynes M. C. "No credit where credit is due: attributional rationalization of women's success in male-female teams." Journal of Applied Psychology. 2005 Sep;90(5):905–16.

Jagsi R., Griffith K. A., Stewart A., Sambuco D., DeCastro R., Ubel P. A. "Gender differences in salary in a recent cohort of early-career physician-researchers." Academic Medicine. 2013 Nov;88(11):1689–99.

Kirwan Institute (2014). "State of the Science: Implicit Bias Review 2014."

Martell, R. F, Guzzo, R. A. (1991). "The dynamics of implicit theories of group performance: When and how do they operate?" Organizational Behavior and Human Decision Processes, 50, 51–74.

Moss-Racusin C. A., Dovidio J. F., Brescoll V. L., Graham M. J., Handelsman J. "Science faculty's subtle gender biases favor male students." Proceedings of the National Academy of Sciences of the United States of America. 2012 Oct 9;109(41):16474–9.

Paradies Y., Priest N., Ben J., Truong M., Gupta A., Pieterse A., Kelaher M., Gee G. "Racism as a determinant of health: a protocol for conducting a systematic review and meta-analysis." Systematic Reviews. 2013 Sep 23;2:85.

Sabin J. A., Greenwald A. G. "The influence of implicit bias on treatment recommendations for 4 common pediatric conditions: pain, urinary tract infection, attention deficit hyperactivity disorder, and asthma." American Journal of Public Health. 2012 May;102(5):988–95.

Stone J, Moskowitz G. B. "Non-conscious bias in medical decision making: what can be done to reduce it?" Medical Education. 2011 Aug;45(8):768–76.

Ran Abramitzky, Leah Platt Boustan, and Katherine Eriksson. (2014). "A Nation of Immigrants: Assimilation and Economic Outcomes in the Age of Mass Migration." Journal of Political Economy. 122(3): 467-506.

Ran Abramitzky, Leah Platt Boustan, and Katherine Eriksson. (2016). "Cultural Assimilation During the Age of Mass Migration." Working paper, and references therein.

Ran Abramitzky, and Leah Platt Boustan. (2016a). "Immigration in American Economic History." NBER Working Paper No. 21882, and references therein.

Vasiliki Fouka. (2015). "Backlash: The Unintended Effects of Language Prohibition in U.S. Schools after World War I." Manuscript.

Allison, M., and Smith, S. (1990). "Leisure and quality of life: Issues facing racial and ethnic minority elderly." Therapeutic Recreation Journal, 24 (3), 50–6.

McCormick, Kate (2007). "The evolution of workplace diversity." Houston Law Review The Department of Labor's Policy & Procedures for Preventing & Eliminating Harassing Conduct in the Workplace (Harassing Conduct Policy) is contained in DLMS 4 — Chapter 700.

2 Faragher v. City of Boca Raton, 524 U.S. 775, 788 (1998).

1. Bertrand, M, Mullainathan, S. "Are Emily And Greg More Employable Than Lakisha And Jamal? A Field Experiment On Labor Market Discrimination." American Economic Review, 2004, v94(4, Sep), 991–1013.

2. Biernat M., Manis M. "Shifting standards and stereotype-based judgments." Journal of Personality and Social Psychology. 1994 Jan;66(1):5–20.

3. Burgess D., van Ryn M., Dovidio J., Saha S. "Reducing racial bias among health care providers: lessons from social-cognitive psychology." Journal of General Internal Medicine. 2007 Jun;22(6):882–7.

4. Carnes M., Devine P. G., Isaac C., Manwell L. B., Ford C. E., Byars-Winston A., Fine E., Sheridan J. T. "Promoting Institutional Change Through Bias Literacy." Journal of Diversity in Higher Education. 2012 Jun;5(2):63–77.

5. Cooper L. A., Roter D. L., Carson K. A., Beach M. C., Sabin J. A., Greenwald A. G., Inui T. S. "The associations of clinicians' implicit attitudes about race with medical visit communication and patient ratings of interpersonal care." American Journal of Public Health. 2012 May;102(5):979–87.

6. Dasgupta, N. (2004). "Implicit Ingroup Favoritism, Outgroup Favoritism, and Their Behavioral Manifestations." Social Justice Research, 17(2), 143–169.

7. Dasgupta, N. (2013). "Implicit Attitudes and Beliefs Adapt to Situations: A Decade of Research on the Malleability of Implicit Prejudice, Stereotypes, and the Self-Concept." Advances in Experimental Social Psychology, 47, 233–279.

8. Dasgupta, N, Greenwald, A. G. (2001). "On the Malleability of Automatic Attitudes: Combating Automatic Prejudice With Images of Admired and Disliked Individuals." Journal of Personality and Social Psychology, 81(5), 800–814.

9. Dore, R. A., Hoffman, K. M., Lillard, A. S. and Trawalter, S. (2014). "Children's racial bias in perceptions of others' pain." British Journal of Developmental Psychology, 32: 218–231.

10. Fiske, S. T. and Taylor, S. E (1991). Social Cognition—International Edition. McGraw-Hill Series in Social Psychology.

11. Glicksman, Eve. "Unconscious Bias in Academic Medicine: Overcoming the Prejudices We Don't Know We Have." Association of American Medical Colleges. 2016 January.

12. Green A. R., Carney D. R., Pallin D. J., Ngo L. H., Raymond K. L., Iezzoni L. I., Banaji M. R. "Implicit bias among physicians and its prediction of thrombolysis decisions for black and white patients." Journal of General Internal Medicine. 2007 Sep;22(9):1231–8.

13. Heilman M. E., Alcott V. B. "What I think you think of me: women's reactions to being viewed as beneficiaries of preferential selection." Journal of Applied Psychology. 2001 Aug;86(4):574–82.

14. Heilman M. E., Haynes M. C. "No credit where credit is due: attributional rationalization of women's success in male-female teams." Journal of Applied Psychology. 2005 Sep;90(5):905–16.

15. Jagsi R., Griffith K. A., Stewart A., Sambuco D., DeCastro R., Ubel P. A. "Gender differences in salary in a recent cohort of early-career physician-researchers." Academic Medicine. 2013 Nov;88(11):1689–99.

16. Kirwan Institute (2014). "State of the Science: Implicit Bias Review 2014."

17. Martell, R. F, Guzzo, R. A. (1991). "The dynamics of implicit theories of group performance: When and how do they operate?" Organizational Behavior and Human Decision Processes, 50, 51–74.

18. Moss-Racusin C. A., Dovidio J. F., Brescoll V. L., Graham M. J., Handelsman J. "Science faculty's subtle gender biases favor male students." Proceedings of the National Academy of Sciences of the United States of America. 2012 Oct 9;109(41):16474–9.

19. Paradies Y., Priest N., Ben J., Truong M., Gupta A., Pieterse A., Kelaher M., Gee G. "Racism as a determinant of health: a protocol for conducting a systematic review and meta-analysis." Systematic Reviews. 2013 Sep 23;2:85.

20. Sabin J. A., Greenwald A. G. "The influence of implicit bias on treatment recommendations for 4 common pediatric conditions: pain, urinary tract infection, attention deficit hyperactivity disorder, and asthma." American Journal of Public Health. 2012 May;102(5):988–95.

21. Stone J, Moskowitz G. B. "Non-conscious bias in medical decision making: what can be done to reduce it?" Medical Education. 2011 Aug;45(8):768–76.

The Department of Labor's Policy & Procedures for Preventing & Eliminating Harassing Conduct in the Workplace (Harassing Conduct Policy) is contained in DLMS 4—chapter 700.

Faragher v. City of Boca Raton, 524 U.S. 775, 788 (1998).

Wedad Andrada Quffa, 2016. "A Review Of The History Of Gender Equality In The United States Of America," Social Sciences and Education Research Review, Department of Communication, Journalism and Education Sciences, University of Craiova, vol. 3(2), pages 143-149

Aurelia DUMITRU & Andrei Bogdan BUDICĂ,, 2017. "Informational Content Of The Periodic Synthesis Reports," Annals of the University of Craiova for Journalism, Communication and Management, Department of Communication, Journalism and Education Sciences, University of Craiova, vol. 3(1), pages 49-61, August.

Bianca Teodorescu, 2017. "The communication between the media and tradition," Social Sciences and Education Research Review, Department of Communication, Journalism and Education Sciences, University of Craiova, vol. 4(2), pages 215-221, December.

01 Jul 2020, Sofia Sprechmann, Secretary-General, Care International

The Global Gender Gap Report 2020, 2022 World Economic Forum

McDonald, L., 2017. Mary Seacole V Florence Nightingale - Nursing Matters. [online] Nursing Matters. Available at: <http://nursing-matters.com/mary-seacole-v-florence-nightingale-2/>

Wonderful Adventures of Mrs. Seacole in Many Lands by Mary Seacole

Printed in the United States
by Baker & Taylor Publisher Services